Gilbert Elliot Minto

The speech of Lord Minto in the House of peers

April 11, 1799

Gilbert Elliot Minto

The speech of Lord Minto in the House of peers
April 11, 1799

ISBN/EAN: 9783337150662

Printed in Europe, USA, Canada, Australia, Japan

Cover: Foto ©ninafisch / pixelio.de

More available books at **www.hansebooks.com**

THE SPEECH

OF

LORD MINTO,

IN THE HOUSE OF PEERS,

APRIL 11, 1799,

ON A

MOTION FOR AN ADDRESS TO HIS MAJESTY,

TO COMMUNICATE

THE RESOLUTIONS

OF

THE TWO HOUSES OF PARLIAMENT,

RESPECTING

AN UNION

BETWEEN

GREAT BRITAIN AND IRELAND.

DUBLIN:

PRINTED BY JOHN EXSHAW, 98, GRAFTON-STREET.

1799.

THE
SPEECH,
&c. &c.

MY LORDS,

IN yielding to the desire, which it is natural for every publick man to feel, of delivering his sentiments on this great question, it could not be my intention, at any period of the discussion, to exhaust, or even to touch on all the many and various points of this comprehensive subject; and I must be yet less disposed to such an attempt in circumstances so little favourable as the present, I mean, after the talents, the learning and the eloquence of two countries have preceded me, and have, indeed, left little for such as me to glean, even in this vast and fertile field.

I shall, therefore, confine myself within bounds better suited to my own capacity, as well as to the measure of indulgence which I can have any pretensions to expect from your Lordships; and shall content myself with stating as clearly, but as shortly as I am able, a few thoughts on the principal and leading topicks of this argument, especially such as have made the strongest impression on my own judgment, and have had the greatest share in determining the opinion I profess in favour of the proposed measure.

In deliberating on this question, the first proposition which seems to impress itself on every mind, is the convenience, amounting indeed to a necessity, not merely for the advantage and benefit, but for the preservation and security of both countries, that there should subsist between Great Britain and Ireland, a close and intimate connexion of one description or other. The most disadvantageous situation in which either country can be placed, is that of total disconnexion. Indeed when I say disadvantageous, I certainly speak too feebly. I mean that this condition would expose both countries to the greatest quantity and variety of evil, and oppose the most in-

surmount-

surmountable barriers to national improvement and prosperity of any that can be imagined. Fundamental as this proposition will be found in the argument, it is nevertheless one on which it is unnecessary to dwell long. I find it, in the first place, conceded on all hands, and I think myself entitled to claim on this point a general or rather universal assent. For I presume it will hardly be required of me, that I should condescend to treat as an exception, worthy of notice, the opinions of those who call themselves United Irishmen, or of those other wretched men, whom the vigilance of Government and of Parliament, has lately exposed to the scorn and execration of a country which they disgrace, under the title of United Englishmen. These men may call themselves by what names they please, United Irish, or United English. In my language they can be known only by the appellation of French Irish, French English. They are merely partizans of the ancient and inveterate enemy of their country. They are wedded to the interests of that enemy, and enlisted under his standard. They are confederates in every desperate and wicked project of a foreign state, for the subjugation and ruin of their native land, and their opinions are entitled

precisely

precisely to the same degree of deference, that we should pay to the sentiments or wishes of the French Directory itself, on a question of British interest. I am, indeed, sorry to learn, that these extremes either of delusion or corruption, should exist in a single instance within the limits of this island: but since such men are, I cannot but observe with satisfaction their hostility to every species of connexion between Great Britain and Ireland, and most of all to that best and most perfect connexion which is now in contemplation. For when I learn from France, and her worthy Irish and English associates, that the present Union between England and Scotland stands in the way of their fraternal views towards Great Britain, and that the union with Ireland is a death's blow to their hopes of annihilating the British empire, I cannot but accept this testimony of the enemy, as the strongest and best confirmation of the favour which I profess, towards the measure which they oppose. But I shall not be expected to argue with this kind of adversary. We are engaged with them in a different sort of controversy, and it is the *ultima ratio* alone that can settle the debate between us. With this exception, however, the necessity of connexion is not only admitted,

ted, but warmly afserted by all those who have taken a part in the debate on this question of Union, whether their judgments have been favourable or adverse to the measure; and your Lordships know that there is no description of persons who have been more earnest to disclaim and abjure the character of what is called separatist, than those who have opposed the Union in Ireland, or in this country.

But if it were not admitted, this proposition is too obvious to require much argument to prove it. A glance on the map, and a moment's reflection will satisfy us, that the affairs and interests of these two sister islands are too much the same, in too many points of domestic and foreign concern, not to associate them necessarily in the dangers and business of war, and in the occupations and pursuits of peace. Let us suppose any one brought from another hemisphere, totally unacquainted, not only with the history and concerns, but even with the shape and form of this quarter of the globe, before whom a map of Europe should be laid for the first time; and let such a man be required to conjecture the distribution of

the

the different countries under his eye, into their respective states and governments. Whatever his opinion might be concerning other portions of Europe, I am persuaded we should all anticipate his confident judgment, that the British Isles, at least, formed one state. Let us, in effect, cast our own eye for an instant on this map—we shall see these two islands not merely contiguous, but lying as it were in the very bosom and embraces of each other—we shall observe, not only their mutual vicinity, but their insulation, and their insulation together, from the rest of Europe; we shall see their relative position with regard to each other and to every other part of the world, and especially their reciprocal dependence, for a secure and undisturbed navigation, in a great part of the circumference of both. These and a thousand other obvious particulars, which I do not enumerate merely to avoid abusing your indulgence with considerations familiar to us all, must convince us, that in a state of total political separation, there could hardly be a single transaction, or an instant of their existence, in which these two countries would not be rivals, and if rivals, enemies. It is easy to conceive the enhanced and aggravated state of warfare waged

waged in this manner between countries pof-
fessing each, in a greater degree, the means
of offence, and in a less degree, those of defence, than in any other possible situation.
We shall also recollect, that if one of these
countries should be engaged in war with a
third, as Great Britain with France, the other
would present advantages to the enemy which
it could not otherwise possess; and it will not
be difficult to foresee, that in a state of separation, the mutual jealousy and habitual ani-
mosity likely to prevail between the neighbours, aided by the intrigues and importunity
of the enemy, will in all probability draw the
neutral island into a direct or indirect participation in these hostilities. Thus will these
two countries, instead of contributing to each
other's comfort, security and greatness, as they
might do under a wiser and happier system,
only harrass, enfeeble, and endanger each
other, just in proportion to their respective
means and resources, exhausting their mutual
attention and energy, rather in watching and
repressing each other, than in repelling common danger, promoting common interests, or
exalting their common greatness and glory.
Such a condition, in a word, disturbs the tran-

B quillity

quillity of peace, and shortens its duration, while it multiplies a thousand fold, the perils and evils of war. It is manifest that the smaller and weaker country of the two, must experience these disadvantages yet more sensibly than its powerful neighbour. In its differences with the other, if the aid and alliance of a third power be sought, that service must be purchased by some consideration or other; and we are taught, by reason as well as history the sort of price that is paid by an inferior, for the proud and politic protection of a powerful state. As the comparatively feeble and poor cannot discharge such a debt in positive force and wealth, it must give what it has, and pay its quota in general subserviency, that is to say, in a base and habitual dependence, little short, either in degradation or ruin, of positive subjection. It appears, in fine, to me, that a smaller country, situated between two great rivals, as Ireland is, can hardly hope for an interval of tranquillity, security or dignity. Dignity may at once be put out of the question, for having no real and positive force to support it, such a country must live, from day to day, by intrigue, the most degrading species of policy, and that which it seems the most impossible

possible to reconcile with any sense of national pride or honour. It can as little look for tranquillity or security; for besides its own quarrels, the causes of which are infinitely multiplied, in a separate state, by that very vicinity which might, otherwise, extinguish them; besides, I say, its own quarrels, it will be dragged perpetually into those of both its neighbours, and will indeed generally find itself the bone of contention, to be worried by both, and to endure therefore that double scourge, that complicated desolation and ruin, which fall on those unhappy countries that are themselves the theatre of wars, in which, perhaps, they have no interest, or none other than that of being themselves the prize to be fought for and destined to reward the conqueror, or purchase the peace of the vanquished. We shall perceive, on the other hand, with the same facility and with greater satisfaction, the inducements and advantages of connexion, by which the resources of the one, instead of being to be substracted from those of the other, flow rather into a general stock, out of which, as from a common heart, strength and prosperity may circulate to the remotest extremities of both, and the right arm of the empire be nourished and fortified, without impoverishing or withering the left. But I will not insist on this conceded point, and shall assume it as a thing proved for granted, that connexion is necessary for the mutual security and happiness of Great Britain and Ireland.

The question then arises, on the best and most eligible mode, or form of that connexion.

On this point also I have a settled opinion, which I consider as a main and principal hinge of this argument. I wish, indeed, to state and to argue it, in the first instance, as a general proposition, but if it be proved, and made out satisfactorily in that form, it seems decisive on that particular question, and will establish, on principle and reason, the same conclusion, to which our judgment may have been led on more practical grounds. The proposition then is this, that when two countries are so circumstanced as mutually to require connexion, the only mode of connexion which can perfectly remove the evils of separation, and fully confer the benefit of union, is a perfect identity and incorporation of their governments. All other relations of a more partial

and

and imperfect nature, are subject to many inconveniences while they subsist, and are besides of limited duration. By limited, I do not mean merely precarious. I consider their expiration not merely as possible or probable, but as certain; and besides the perpetual and restless struggles, which are for ever vexing these contentious relations while they last, they appear to me to possess this fundamental and characteristic vice: I mean that of tending gradually, and though perhaps not always rapidly, yet certainly and inevitably, by the very law of their constitution and nature, to a total extinction and dissolution. Nations, then, connected in this manner, will necessarily arrive, at one period or other, at the alternative of separation, towards which they naturally tend, involving, probably, mutual and perpetual hostility, or that perfect incorporation and unity, which is productive not only of all the blessings of internal tranquillity, but of all the advantages, both in strength and prosperity, which flow from the union of their joint resources, and which are encreased, by combination, far beyond the simple addition to their amount.

That such are the properties and defects of
these

these imperfect connexions, we shall easily satisfy ourselves, by a very short and cursory view of one or two of the principal relations of that description, and I shall begin with that which I conceive to stand first, also, in chronological order—I mean conquest. For I believe it will generally be found, when two countries are situated in such a manner as to invite, by their local positions, a connexion between their governments, the stronger of the two, or that which is first enabled by an earlier civilization, and superior population, to aim at foreign enterprise, will attempt the conquest of the other, and if the attempt succeeds, that mode of relation is established between them, which I am now treating of. Conquest may, indeed, in one sense, be understood to expressonly the means employed for uniting them under one government, or bringing them together, and in that acceptation, conquest may, no doubt, lead to any mode of connexion, and, amongst the rest, may tend at once to that which is the most perfect and the best. Of this, indeed, history will furnish examples, though, I believe, not frequent; for war is but a rough courtship, and violence cannot be expected, in all cases, to procure so happy an union as that which, at once, incorporated the Roman and the Sabine people.

people. At present, however, I use the word conquest to express, not the means or instrument of union, but the relation which is the consequence of victory, and which subsists after it. In other words, I mean that dominion which is exercised by the conqueror on the title of conquest, while the countries continue distinct; or that sovereignty, which being founded by the sword, is measured by the power of enforcing it, on one hand, and the inability to resist, on the other. In comparing, as we are now doing, the advantages and disadvantages of the different kinds of connexion between nations, we may, no doubt, dismiss at once from the argument the consideration of conquest; for I presume we shall agree that this is the worst of all. It is, indeed, the most wretched condition of human slavery. The relation of master and servant, or even of master and slave, amongst individuals, or of sovereign and subject amongst the members of one commonwealth, even under the most despotick forms of government, may be conceived to produce, at least in some instances, or in some degree, a mutual benefit and convenience. But it is not so amongst nations. A master nation will, I think, generally be found a tyrant, and a subject nation is generally a slave. The submission

and

and obedience of the one does not purchafe protection or kindnefs, and the authority of the other yields little profit. The dominion of mere conqueft, in a word, confers on the fovereign but a barren fceptre and a crown of thorns; and very fit it fhould be fo. Yet under all thefe difcouragements it will generally be found, that a ftrong fenfe of the evils attending feparation, ftimulated perhaps by that paffion, I mean ambition, which feems to actuate all governments, or thofe who adminifter them, will induce the ftronger power to feek connexion by that courfe, unlefs precluded by the eftablifhment of fome better or lefs objectionable mode of relation.

Amongft thefe I fhall next fpeak of federal connexion, and I am the more inclined to fay a few words on that fubject, as I have underftood that, in the variety of opinions entertained on this queftion of Union with Ireland, fome have been fuppofed to lean towards a connexion of that nature. I confefs, however, that I can find nothing in that mode of relation to recommend it; and every thing we know of fuch confederacies feems to prove them, in the firft place, inadequate to the purpofes of union,

union, and, in the next place, of very precarious duration. The fundamental vice of these federal constitutions seems to be, that professing to provide only for some common interests, they not only leave, but it is, in some sort, their spirit to establish, a distinctness, and even an opposition of interests on all or many other points. Speaking of national interests, I believe it will be safe to consider distinctness as in general but a convertible term for opposition; and the different parts of a federal union are, I think, generally to be accounted rivals in respect of all in which they are distinct. Their opposition is indeed not limited even by that principle, but extends often to the very *fœdus fœderis*; I mean to those concerns which are common, and the general interest in which is meant to be provided for by the conditions and obligations of the union. It must be observed by every one who reads the history of such governments, that in the interpretation and performance of their federal engagements, the parties generally act in a spirit of rival and adverse contention. The passions of the multitude seem to flow naturally in that course; and the narrow genius of those why will often have the lead in
the

the discordant counsels of such states, seems prone enough to fall in with this popular humour. We shall frequently observe them more occupied in the internal jealousies and competitions of the confederate states, than in promoting the common cause; and especially in moments of common danger and exertion, they will often discover a greater apprehension of contributing a grain too much in the federal scale, than a grain too little for the success of that object, which is the only rational motive for exertion at all. They are, in a word, more afraid of giving some paltry advantage to a friend and associate, than solicitous to defeat the common enemy, or to provide for common safety. Irrational as this conduct is, I may appeal to observation and history for the existence as well as for the fatal effects of this mania, both in federal governments, and in the looser and yet more temporary and occasional confederacies of mere allies. We have ourselves lived in a very eventful period, and have had but too large an experience in revolutions of every sort. We have, amongst others, witnessed the recent downfal of a great federal government; I mean the United Provinces: and I certainly agree with what I understood to be

the

the sentiment of a noble Lord who opened this discussion on a former day, in thinking that the sudden and rapid overthrow of that government, and the degrading ruin and slavery into which that celebrated people has been plunged almost without a struggle, may be traced to the very vice and defect in the constitution of such governments which I have just described. It is surely reasonable to doubt, whether a more prompt and combined application of the resources which that country possessed, than, it seems, the distinctness and contrariety of its parts admitted of, might not have averted, at least the easy and inglorious conquest of a country, whose accidental and temporary union under the extraordinary talents of the great Prince of Orange, was able first to defy, and then to humble and defeat France, in the plenitude of Louis the Fourteenth's power and greatness. I shall probably not differ with many of your Lordships in ascribing, at least in part, to the same cause, the sudden calamities which have overwhelmed another brave and respectable people, I mean the Swiss cantons, with a rapidity and ease, which can be accounted for only on that principle. And I cannot suppress some apprehension that we may yet have to lament, even in our own day, the dissolution of the grandest confederacy which the world ever knew, the integrity of which has already been too much broken not to excite anxiety and alarm for the issue, and on the stability of which, however, not only rests the safety and happiness of those extensive territories, and of the many nations which have hitherto found security and shelter under that great union, but I may say, perhaps, on which the independence and liberty of the whole of Europe, and a great proportion of the other three quarters of the globe, may essentially and eventually depend. I speak, my Lords, of the Germanic body itself. But I will dwell no longer on these unpleasant topics, not immediately applicable to the question of the day, and hasten to the consideration of that species of relation which is the proper subject of your present deliberation; I mean that which now subsists between Great Britain and Ireland, and which did subsist between England and Scotland before the Union.

I am to speak now of those connexions which consist in some circumstance of identity, in the municipal constitutions of the two countries; that is to say, in having some

part

part or member of their governments the same, with a diftinctnefs and feparate independence in all the reft. Such is that of one King or Executive Power, with feparate legiflatures; and of this particular form of connexion we have undoubtedly had moft experience in this empire, and can therefore fpeak of it with the beft information and knowledge. I might, no doubt, fafely appeal, at once, to that very experience, for the infufficiency of fuch a bond, to avoid the evils of diftinct exiftence, or to confer, in peace or war, the full benefits of connexion. But I wifh, firft, to fay a few words to what may be confidered as the principle; that is to fay, to enquire what are the circumftances from which the evils of thefe partial relations may be thought to flow; and above all, what is the true caufe of that natural and conftant tendency in fuch governments, to weaken and diminifh the bonds of connexion, till it becomes little more than nominal, and remains, perhaps, only perceptible in the ftruggles and convulfions of its diffolution.

The firft defect, then, which I remark in this mode of imperfect connexion, is fimilar, or perhaps I may fay, precifely the fame, with that

which

which I have already observed upon, in relations merely federal. I mean that the connexion being but partial, and intended for partial purposes, the great mass of interests in each nation continue distinct; the attention of each country is still pointed towards a separate view of individual interest; and the public mind, if I may so express it, of the two nations, is kept distinct. I have already observed that distinct interests are generally opposite interests, or felt to be so by the two parties; and speaking of nations, I may add, that distinct minds are generally hostile. In these circumstances, the vicinity, and the connexion of such countries, instead of improving, as they might otherwise do, friendship and harmony between them, seem to produce the very opposite effects, and to cultivate a jealous and angry temper, prone to take offence and umbrage, and ripening every trivial discontent or difference into grounds of permanent alienation and even hostility.

Another grand source of indisposition between such countries, and that from which every one of the evils attending this mode of relation seems to me most immediately to derive, is the inequality in their relative power and influence, occasioned, no doubt, by their

inequality

inequality in real and positive power and influence. It follows necessarily from the very nature and constitution of human affairs, and no artificial or conventional arrangement, no provisions of positive institution can alter it, that in the union of two distinct and unequal countries, the superior must be predominant, and the inferior subordinate in their common concerns, and in the administration of the common parts of their Government. Hence follows, however, a nominal independence in the inferior state, accompanied by a daily and irksome consciousness of real dependence and subordination. It is this contradiction between the real and nominal condition of the inferior country that I consider as the most fruitful source of those evils which afflict such connexions, and ultimately extinguish them. In Governments administered in this manner, under external influence, the eyes of the nation pass over the immediate and domestic instruments of their administration, to that which must appear to them, and may indeed be truly accounted its efficient head, I mean the external power which directs it's counsels. It is therefore natural that the grievances, real or imaginary of such a country,

try, should be laid to the account of that higher cause; that it's discontents, chagrins, and resentments should be directed against that object; and that the exertions of patriotism, or the struggles of faction, as the case may be, the clamour and the activity, the eloquence and even the virtues of popular leaders and ambitious men, should all aim at that obvious mark. They will find in the people a disposition, founded also in nature, extremely favourable to the success of such aims. I have said that the minds of two countries thus circumstanced are not only distinct, but hostile. Jealousy is the sentiment likely to prevail between them; and indeed where both being nominally, and according to their abstract rights, independent and equal, one of the two exercises, nevertheless, a clear and undisguised ascendency over the other, jealousy may, in truth, be thought to have no very unreasonable foundation. The prevailing national sentiment, the ruling passion, then, of the inferior country, comes to be an angry, impatient and intolerant love of their independency. Whoever touches that string, reaches their heart, and commands their affections and actions. Hence we shall observe a

restless

restless and never satisfied struggling with every circumstance either in the constitution of their government, or in the counsels and measures of their administration, which seems, even to the most subtle refinements of jealousy, to affect that object; hence a perpetual straining after its improvement and perfection; and hence also those imprudent, and, surely, ungenerous advantages which are sought, in periods of common distress or danger, to extort concessions favourable to that object; concessions which do not excite gratitude in those who receive them, because they are claimed as rights and seem to have been enforced by necessity; concessions too which seem rather to whet than to satisfy the appetite that calls for them. Each victory of this kind becomes only a vantage ground from whence another may be sought for; and thus each succession of patriots, or of demagogues, seeking to enhance on the exploits of their predecessors, the improvement of indepedency is pushed forward until the true goal of that course comes in view —I mean separation.

That separation is in truth the goal or winning post of this race of independency, must appear very clearly when we consider what the fundamental cauſe of the ſubordination complained of is, and what therefore muſt be the means of reducing it. The aſcendancy of the ſuperior country conſiſts, no doubt, in it's ſuperior power, but it is the conſtitutional connexion that furniſhes the channel or organ, through which the power of the ſuperior ſtate is brought home to the inferior country. If they have the ſame executive power, the influence of the ſuperior ſtate operates through that channel on every branch and department of publick affairs. If their legiſlatures, diſtinct in other reſpects, have one branch or member in common, the legiſlation of the inferior is bent to uniformity with the other by that power. Connexion then is the means of aſcendancy in one, and the cauſe of ſubordination in the other, and it is manifeſt that theſe grievances can be alleviated, or redreſſed, only by diminiſhing or aboliſhing the cauſe. That is to ſay, in other words, that independency can be improved only by ſtriking off, link after link, of the connexion, and it's entire perfection can be attained only by breaking the laſt thread which holds the countries together.

From this account of the matter it appears unavoidable that the courſe I have deſcribed ſhould

should be pursued in every similar case, and that these events are not to be considered as fortuitous, but as deriving from uniform and pregnant causes likely to produce the same consequences wherever they exist. We are taught, then, not less by reason, than, as we shall soon find, by experience, to expect that the natural and commendable love of independence on one hand, and the incompatibility of that independence with connexion on the other, should always lead two countries thus circumstanced to the last alternative, which I have already more than once alluded to, of separation or union; an alternative in which I am persuaded that true wisdom, and a sincere and genuine love of our country, will always make one choice, while passion and prejudice, especially private passion or prejudice, and while a blind and sophisticated pride, personating, or rather counterfeiting patriotism, may possibly prompt another.

If I have not been deceived by this reasoning, one might almost venture, without much temerity, to trace, as the pretty certain and uniform succession and progress of events, in the history of connexion between two neighbouring countries of unequal power, the course I have just described. Their connexion will probably begin in conquest—that miserable condition will gradually soften itself into some mode of dependent connexion. This will still be refined into the more flattering condition of nominal independence, accompanied, however, by a real and inherent subordination;--under which the uneasiness of the subordinate country, and its growing pretensions and power, will advance in the progress towards real independence, till it approaches so closely the danger of seperation, that both countries will be alarmed, and take shelter from the impending calamity, in the only sanctuary that remains, I mean Union. I will not say that every step in this progress will be the same in all cases. The events, such of them as happen, will probably succeed each other in the same order; but a link or two more may be found in some instances, and a link or two may be omitted in others. I think myself, however, supported not only by such reasoning as I have ventured to lay before you, but by the uniform testimony of history, at least in this observation; I mean that a partial connexion of Government, between two unequal countries, is not a permanent condition

tion in which they can settle, and is incapable of subsisting long without change; that it is not a stationary point, but merely transitory and progressive, and is but a stage or resting place, if that which I have described as constantly progressive can obtain the name of rest at all, between the original state of total disconnexion, from which they started, and either a return to that total separation again, or that which I consider as the more probable term of its Progress, even on the first approach of that evil, but is ultimately certain, I mean perfect and entire consolidation and union.

I profess myself so strongly impressed with this view, I will not say of the philosophical principal, but of history and experience applicable to the subject we are considering, that I cannot help looking to the union of Great Britain and Ireland, not merely as an advantageous and desirable event, and on that account likely to bring itself about, but as certain and unavoidable, although I shall take care not to commit my philosophy too rashly, by assigning any particular period, whether long or short, for the accomplishment of its predictions. I assert only that we are travelling that road. These two countries are visibly approaching
each

each other by an irresistible attraction, by a species of gravitation which I consider as an invincible law of political nature, if nature can have such an epithet; and that closing, as it were, by the compulsion of this power, no human obstruction, no counterpoise that can be opposed to it, will long avail to keep them asunder, though it may retard their meeting for a while. I am not less persuaded that when once they are in contact, another principal, equally inherent in that new condition, I mean a principle of inseparable adhesion and tenacity, will hold them together, and will so cement and consolidate their union, as to render all human efforts to seperate and tear them again asunder, vain and ineffectual. If these opinions then have any foundation, we may debate here concerning the best means of accelerating this happy and much to be desired event, but we may consider the event itself as perdestined; and I cannot help persuading myself that the species of destiny, of which I am here speaking, I mean the steady operation of fixed principles, will work out its own decrees, be the process longer or shorter; and neither that erroneous pride, which is supposed to pervade Ireland in general, nor the love of political monopoly, which may actuate particular

classes

classes, or individuals of that country; nor the arts, the seductions, or the arms of the French Republick, can be long interposed between the cause and its effect, or disturb for ever the appointed order of human events, by constraining Great Britain and Ireland to endure the afflictions and calamities of seperation, or of a condition almost equivalent to it, while they contemplate all the blessings of Union placed within their reach, and courting their acceptance.

With this view of the necessity and inevitable nature of this event, the opinion I entertain of its utility is at least consoling to my own mind. Yet I should neither have hazarded such speculations, nor have presumed to detain your Lordships, especially so long, with this sort of reasoning, if I had thought it no better than idle and visionary theory. But, in truth, I was conscious that it was history rather than speculation that I was delivering throughout, and I will venture to say there is hardly a point or turn in this speculative course, which you will not find verified, chapter for chapter, by the history of every connexion we have hitherto known with the nations which now compose our empire.

Your

your Lordships will think me difposed to carry you far back, when I venture even to name the Saxon heptarchy, and the union of thofe feven independent kingdoms in the reign of Egbert. Yet if I do little more than allude to that fignal event, it is not becaufe I am wanting, or that I can think your Lordfhips fo, in a due fenfe of its importance and dignity, or of its influence on the fubfequent deftinies either of England or of the world. It is enough to fay that the union of the heptarchy was the birth day of nothing lefs than this very kingdom of England, and that the glorious empire which now extends from eaft to weft, and has planted the dominion and the language of England around the globe, is the lineal defcendant, or rather only the natural growth and developement of that event. It is not my intention, however, to dwell on this antient and parent union, for the purpofe of illuftrating the principles of which I have juft treated. I am fenfible that this period is too remote from our own, to build any folid conclufion on tranfactions, with the details and particulars of which we are fo little acquainted. I therefore mention it only that I may be entitled to read a fhort paffage from Mr. Hume's hiftory of that

that period, which, I think, may furnish a reflection or two not impertinent to the present question.

"The kingdoms of the heptarchy, though
"united by so recent a conquest, seemed to be
"so strongly cemented into one state under
"Egbert; and the inhabitants of the several
"provinces had lost all desire of revolting from
"that conqueror, or of restoring their indepen-
"dent Governments. Their language was every
"where nearly the same; their customs, laws,
"institutions, civil and religious; and as the
"race of their antient Kings was totally ex-
"tinct in all their subjected states, the people
"readily transferred their allegiance to a Prince
"who seemed to merit it, by the splendour of
"his victories, the vigour of his administra-
"tion, and the superior nobility of his birth.
"An union also in government opened to
"them the agreeable prospect of future tran-
"quillity; and it appeared more probable,
"that they would thenceforth become terri-
"ble to their neighbours, than be exposed to
"their inroads and devastations." We collect from this passage, not merely as an opinion of Mr. Hume's, but as an historical fact,

E that

that the local attachment and national feeling which the inhabitants of the several independent kingdoms before their union entertained, no doubt, towards their respective countries, were easily and quickly extended to the whole united kingdom. This change did not even wait for a new generation, but was operated in the very life of the conqueror, and therefore of those who were themselves habituated to the narrower feeling, and who had experienced in their own persons the humiliation and resentment belonging to defeat. For it is also remarkable that the harmonizing property of union was manifested in circumstances the most adverse of any to conciliation, I mean in the case of an union brought about by force, and attended with all the irritation of compulsion and conquest. We must observe, in the next place, that Mr. Hume considers a similarity of language, customs, laws, and institutions, civil and religious, as circumstances, favourable, not only to the establishment of union, but to the improvement and promotion of its beneficial consequences. And lastly, we have the authority of this profound and philosophical historian for thinking that such an union was likely not

only

only to yield the comforts of internal tranquillity and peace, but fo to improve the power and refources of the kingdom, as, inftead of trembling at the approach of every invader, to render it rather itfelf an object of terror, or at leaft, of refpect to furrounding nations. It is true that the Danifh invafions followed immediately on this event, and we know that the repeated and powerful defcents of that warlike nation, not only harraffed and alarmed this ifland upwards of a century, but at fome periods reduced the Saxon power to the greateft poffible ftreights. But in the firft place, the Danifh invafions were not the confequence of the union of the Heptarchy, and muft have happened without it. And in the next place, it is impoffible to read the hiftory of that period without perceiving, in every page a demonftration of the falutary effects of that meafure, and without afcribing to the union under Egbert, alone, the ultimate prefervation of that kingdom. If the Danes had found the ifland in the fame feeble and divided ftate, in which the Saxons had themfelves atchieved the conqueft of the Britons; if they had had to contend only with the disjointed, difunited, and fingle exertions of the feven infignificant

E 2   States

States of the Heptarchy each in its turn, and if those Princes who fought for England had not been enabled by the union to oppose to this powerful and persevering enemy a combined and concerted defence, it is manifest that neither the valour and talents of Egbert, nor the almost romantick endowments and virtues of Alfred the Great, would have availed to prevent a conquest as complete, and an extirpation of the Saxon power and name out of England, as perfect and dreadful as that which they had themselves inflicted on the defenceless and divided Britons. But to pass forward to times somewhat nearer our own, I would now speak of Wales.

Wales had resisted the power of all the Saxon Kings, and the first Princes of the Norman line. It was not till the reign of Henry the Third, and then rather by the effect of internal dissention, than by the arms or enterprize of that Prince, that Wales was brought under a sort of feudal dependance on the Crown of England, and acknowledged the Sovereign of the latter country as a feudal superior. Wales was held, then, during that reign meerly as a fief, with the usual acknowledg-

ments,

ments, and under the ufual conditions belonging to the feudal relation of feignory and vaffalage, but without any claim on the part of England to political fovereignty. This flender relation feems, however, to have improved itfelf very rapidly into a connexion of a different and much more intimate nature, for in the very next reign, Edward the Firft, the immediate fucceffer of Henry the Third, was able to convert that feudal feigneury into direct and pofitive fovreignty, and to annex the Principality of Wales infeparably, and as part of the dominion of the Crown, to the throne of England. At the fame period, and indeed on that occafion, a partial communication, and but a partial one, of the laws and police of England was made to Wales, by the *Statum Walliæ*, as it is called, in the twelfth year of the reign of Edward the Firft. I mention thefe particulars only to obferve, that at this period commenced an æra of connexion between England and Wales, not indeed precifely the fame in all points, but bearing, however, fome refemblance and analogy to that which we are principally confidering to-day. I mean an imperfect political connexion, which confifted in the two countries being governed by the fame
Prince,

Prince, with a partial uniformity of laws and inftitutions, remaining diftinct and feparate in other refpects.

If we would appreciate the value of fuch a connexion, and its efficacy in producing either internal tranquility or external peace, we have only to purfue the hiftory of that connexion, throughout the whole period of its duration, from the reign of Edward the Firft to that of Henry the Eighth. It is by no means my intention to interrupt this debate by fuch a narrative, but merely to direct your Lordfhip's attention to the refult of fuch an enquiry. For your Lordfhips know that Wales was not only difquieted within, by the troubles and turbulence of civil diforder, but that both countries were afflicted by a perpetual fucceffion of mutual inroads and petty warfare, not perhaps of fufficient dignity to attract the notice of general hiftory, but fufficient to keep them both expofed to the frequent calamities, and the conftant anxiety attending a ftate of permanent hoftility with a neighbouring enemy, and by thefe means retard and interrupt on both fides of the border, but efpecially in Wales, the progrefs of civilization, of arts,

of

of industry, of wealth, and, in a word, of public improvement in all its branches. But this was a state of things, which, as I have said, could not last for ever, and the only perfect and sovereign remedy for such disorders, was at length administered in the reign of Harry the Eighth, by that incorporating legislative Union which extinguished in a day the discord of ages, and identified forever these two not only distinct, but hostile nations. In our enquiry then concerning the comparative advantages or disadvantages of these two modes of relation, I mean that imperfect one which proposes to combine connexion with distinctness, and that perfect legislative Union which confounds and incorporates both the nations and their governments, we have only to compare, or rather to contrast, the uneasy and afflicting period which preceded the Union in the reign of Harry the Eighth, with the two centuries of mutual security and peace, and of progressive and still increasing prosperity and happiness, power, splendour and dignity which have succeeded, and as it is reasonable to conclude, have derived in a great degree, if not principally, from that event.

England

England felt very early the advantage of connexion with *Scotland*; and projects for uniting them, even on the best principle of Union, were set on foot, and repeated in various forms, and on the slightest prospects of success, from the earliest period down to the very latest, that is to say, to the actual accomplishment of that salutary design. But such purposes, wise and beneficial as they are, must, it seems, mature themselves in the fullness of time; and although it is ordained that these events shall happen, they must happen, it would seem, in their due and appointed order. It will be found, I believe, that neighbouring nations will seldom begin with union, though they are sure to end with it. The work of connexion commenced, then also, in this case, at the natural beginning of the process, and conquest was resorted to as the instrument of union. This part of the Scotch course, however, was never atchieved. Scotland never was conquered. But the attempt, and all the miseries attending that long and obstinate struggle, deluged both countries in blood, and during more than three centuries afflicted them with calamities, the amount of which, on either side,

historians

historians can hardly report faithfully, without the charge of exaggeration. This fanguinary and ruinous contest terminated in the Union of the Crowns, at the accession of James the first; and here commenced a century of that precise relation which is the subject of our present enquiry. The two kingdoms had one Prince, and one Executive Power, with separate Parliaments. Scotland asserted a perfect independence and equality, but experienced a real subordination. It would, undoubtedly, be unfair, if I were to impute to this cause alone, the many disadvantages under which Scotland appears to have laboured, and the declining condition of that country which is observed by historians during the period I have mentioned. Much of the calamity which fell upon both kingdoms, must be placed to the account of the troubles and civil wars to which every part of the island partook during a great proportion of the last century, and which, amongst other extraordinary events produced, under the Commonwealth, a hasty and short-lived, because ill digested and ill conceived, Union of the three kingdoms of England, Scotland and Ireland. But with all these allowances, it is not the less true, that the last century was a period of great political difcord and diffention between England and Scotland, in which the latter country entertained and manifefted, as we have been led to expect, that angry and querulous temper which I have defcribed as growing out of the fituation, and as infeparable from that jarring and abhorrent union of nominal independence and real fubordination. This caufe produced its natural effects, and both difturbed the empire in peace, and weakened it in war, fometimes by political contention between the people of Scotland and the Monarch, fometimes by the habitual animofity of the two countries, hardly kept under by the authority or mediation of the common fovereign, fometimes by the intrigues of Scotland with France, and above all by the purfuit of the idol independence, to the very brink of feparation. The very unity of the Crowns became a grievance; and your Lordfhips know, that towards the clofe of this period, I mean in the firft years of the reign of Queen Anne and of the prefent century, partly by projects for abridging the perogative, becaufe it was adminiftered out of Scotland, partly by projects for ufurping a confiderable portion of the regal power, in order that it might

might be administered within Scotland; partly, in fine, by refusing to accede to the settlement of the succession adopted in England, the Parliament of Scotland, the patriots of Scotland, with the acclamation of the whole people of Scotland, brought the danger of impending separation so home to the sense and bosoms of both countries, that their prudence was at length alarmed; they opened their arms to each other, and took shelter from imminent and incurable ruin, in that inseparable embrace which has ever since, and I trust ever will, continue to unite us. It is thus that extremes touch, and thus that these two nations, from the last term of alienation and repugnance, passed at a single step, into the closest and most indissoluble union.

The connexion between England and Ireland began in conquest, and the relation was that of sovereign and subject. I do not say a sovereign able, at all times, to enforce his dominion, or a submissive subject acknowledging and acquiescing under the authority of his master. But whatever connexion subsisted between the two countries, had that origin and preferved that character through its firſt period. This firſt and intolerable ſtage of national relation paſſed forward, however, and foftened itſelf gradually, but through the fanguinary procefs of habitual refiſtance and infubordination, fwelling occafionally into civil wars and rebellions of the moſt ferocious character, into a dependent connexion, or a mitigated but avowed dependence of Ireland on England. I allude now to that period during which the Iriſh nation, with a parliament of their own, were, however, fubject to the legiſlature of England. I do not fpeak of the *right*, nor wiſh to engage in that already obfolete, though recent controverfy. I fpeak only of the *fact*, for fuch was the conſtitution, *de facto*, of Engliſh and Iriſh connexion, in the memory of the youngeſt of your Lordſhips. This fecond period, alfo, paſſed away, and the prefent improved ſtate of Iriſh independence, as it now fubfiſts, was atchieved by means, which I have already had occafion to allude to; I mean by the opportune exertion of Iriſh energy in moments of Britiſh debility and diftrefs. For thofe conceſſions were certainly granted in circumſtances of durefs, whether they may now, with better grace, be ſtated to

have

have flowed from the juftice and liberal difpofition of the conceding country, or not. In the mean while we have arrived, in the due and regular courfe, at that precife point of connexion, which has been the principal object of difcuffion. We have a common prince, with feparate parliaments. Ireland claims a fovereign independent government, and that claim is freely admitted by our own; while we exercife, neverthelefs, with the acquiefcence of Ireland, an open afcendancy and controul in every one of its concerns. We are at this moment, therefore, making an experiment, which is not yet twenty years old, of the mutual advantages to be derived from that mode of connexion, of its efficacy in ftrengthening the empire, in repelling danger from without, in reconciling the minds and affections of the nations within, and, finally, in cementing and perpetuating their union. We muft, indeed, regard the prefent moment as the firft, in which the courfe of events has furnifhed the proper ordeal of this condition; I mean a crifis of difficulty and danger to the empire; for this is the true touchftone on which the virtue of connexion and of mutual engagements may be proved. Surely, my
Lords,

Lords, at this period of the argument, I may claim the benefit of facts, of which we are ourselves the living witnesses, and appeal at once to the disastrous testimony of the present hour, not only for the inadequacy of such a system to yield protection and support in the period of difficulty, but for its active and fatal efficacy in augmenting the danger and hastening the common ruin. Can we need better proof than every tide has of late brought us, that the present feeble and flimsy bond which connects Great Britain with Ireland, does not possess one principle of stability, and has not stamina to resist that innate tendency to decay and dissolution, which accompanies all life from the cradle, whether natural or politick. What result then is it reasonable to look for from this experiment? I should wish to speak on this occasion, not merely with respect, but I must say, with gratitude and reverence, of the conduct held by that which we must call the Irish nation, and which is, indeed, entitled to that appellation. I mean the Irish Government, the Irish Parliament, a great portion of the property of Ireland, of its gentry, and even of its people. In these we have witnessed exertions of courage, activity, perseverance, and

spirit,

spirit, as well as of fidelity and honour, in fulfilling the engagements of their connexion with us, and in the protection and defence of their own country, which challenge the thanks of Great Britain, and the approbation of the world. But this sentiment cannot either conceal from us, or disguise other truths, not less obvious, though less grateful and welcome. The loyalty, the prudence, and spirit, which we commend, on one hand, do not, however, prevent an extensive and desperate conspiracy, on the other, against the common safety of Great Britain and Ireland, and aiming, above all, avowedly and distinctly against that connexion, in which the safety of both is felt to reside. After hearing his Majesty's lawful exercise of the powers with which the Constitution of Ireland has invested him, and the legitimate means employed by the Sovereign of that country to preserve a uniformity of measures in the direction of our common interests, treated as the interference of a foreign power, we have the misfortune of seeing at this hour a great portion of the Irish people, considerable for its numbers, and, I fear, not altogether contemptible, even for its blood and talents, in open rebellion against our common Sovereign,

reign, and in clofe alliance with our common enemy. The diffolution of all connexion between us is the object they profefs. The grievance which they have rifen to redrefs is that connexion; the caufe which their manifeftos proclaim, the ftandard under which they mufter and fight, is feparation. This end then, towards which we have feen fuch connexions are continually prone, this very feparation, which is the natural inborn propenfity of imperfect relation, is already, in this cafe, the fubject of a cival war, and is at this moment committed to the iffue of arms, which is ftill depending. I have glanced, in this manner, the hiftory of Britifh and Irifh connexion only to fhew, that amongft its many other evils, that of tendency to total extinction, which we have been taught by principle, and by the example of other countries, to expect, is proved in fact, and in the actual cafe, to be one of its properties; and I am hardly apprehenfive of a diffenting voice to the conclufion which appears to me to refult from this deduction, whether of hiftory or reafon, that we have reached the point at which, in the firft place, the evils of imperfect connexion are at their height, and in the next, beyond which lies only that alternative,

fo

so often mentioned, of separation or union. We stand precisely in that predicament, in which the prudence of both countries, and the fidelity and honour of those who are entrusted with their interests, I mean their Governments and Legislatures, are called upon by the most solemn and instant appeal, I mean the peril of their countries, to snatch them from that precipice, on the very edge of which they stand, already wavering, and too giddy to save themselves. It cannot, surely, be a difficult or doubtful question, whether we should fold our arms, and look on upon this danger, and the certain ruin in which it ends, or follow that secure and already trodden path which has already conducted two other countries, now identified with England, I mean Wales and Scotland, to more than safety. We have surely learnt from both those examples, that the measure adopted by them, not only affords a perfect remedy against the evils with which we are now contending, but possesses precisely the opposite property from that which is the character of our present imperfect, ill-constructed connexion; namely, that of tending to a constant and certain improvement and perfection, instead of diminution and deterioration

deterioration of union and all its beneficial fruits.

Having hitherto treated the queſtion ſomewhat ſpeculatively, I would now ſpeak more particularly to the practical inducements which ſhould recommend this meaſure to both countries; and, firſt, to Great Britain.

The advantages to be derived to Great Britain from an incorporating union with Ireland may be divided into poſitive and negative.

By poſitive, I mean an acceſſion of real and efficient force to our preſent Empire, as a navel and military power; for were all cauſe of difference between the countries extinguiſhed, and were the affections of the whole of Ireland as ſincerely directed towards the general ſervice of the Empire, and its force as diſpoſable for that purpoſe, as may be ſaid of every part of Great Britain, it cannot be doubted that the power and reſources of that Empire would receive an eſſential augmentation and improvement. But I would rather paſs on to that claſs of advantage which I have called negative, and which appears to me the moſt material of the two.

By

By the negative advantage of union, I mean that of avoiding, in moments of war and difficulty, thofe embarraffments which have never failed to diftract and annoy us as often, at leaft of late years, as war and difficulty have occurred, and which render Ireland, at this moment, inftead of a refource, only a dead weight hung round the neck of Britifh exertion, at a time when the full energy of both might be well employed againft the common enemy. The cafe is fuch, that we have not only to contend with this difficulty in our conteft with France, but it muft, I think, be an improvident and fanguine view of our own affairs, and of the general events in Europe, to confider even the prefervation of Ireland, I mean her prefervation to the paternal government of his Majefty, and the continuance of any connexion between us, as a matter which is not become, in fome degree or other, problematical and precarious. I would by no means be underftood to fpeak defpondently on that fubject; I am far from feeling fo. I fpeak only of danger and doubt, as exciting a prudent exertion to counteract them, not of a mean or unprofitable fear. No man in England can repofe a more entire confidence in

the vigilance, the skill and the divine valour of the British navy than myself. I profess an equal reliance on the courage and discipline of British troops, endowed as I have always thought them with higher excellence than those of any other nation in the world. I have a firm confidence also in the spirit and bravery of the Irish nation, and in the honour and fidelity of that part of it which professes attachment to our empire, and to our mutual connexion; but with all these grounds of rational hope and expectation, there are two points in which I cannot feel the same implicit confidence, on each of which, however, our ultimate security, and the issue of this contest must depend. I cannot rely confidently on the constancy of fortune in war; nor on the steadiness and uniformity of any national sentiment whatever. I do not know why there is a rebellion in Ireland at all. I have never heard any adequate cause assigned for it. Such pretences as have been resorted to for justifying it, have either been posterior to the events of which they are alledged to have been the causes; or utterly irreconcileable with the avowed objects of the rebellion. Who for example will believe those
men

men sincere who would ascribe their insurrection to the religious differences between two sects of christians, while they propose to redress that grievance, by a remedy, the success of which must eradicate from their country, or subject to a furious and fanatic persecution, the profession of christianity itself? I have never, I say, heard any distinct grievance articulated, which would not be enhanced a thousand fold, by the most perfect success that can be proposed in the acknowledged objects of this absurd rebellion. Not knowing then the principle of the present troubles in Ireland, I have no rule for measuring their extent, or for limiting their progress, and I cannot say with confidence, whether any part of the Irish nation, or at least the greater and predominant part, will at some future period even profess adherence to British connexion; neither am I endowed with the means of predicting positively the event of another enterprize against Ireland, if the enemy should attempt it in more favourable circumstances. I repeat it, my Lords, I do not despond on this view of the danger; I say on the contrary that the proper means are sure to repel it. I speak only of the danger as of a motive for

exerting

exerting both wifdom and courage in oppofing it. In that view I am conftrained to acknowledge doubt, and doubt on fuch a queftion cannot be divefted of anxiety, nor feparated from a duty to aim at the attainment of better fecurity for objects of fuch unappreciable value. I do not fay Ireland muft be loft if we have not a Union, but I cannot fay lefs than this, that we have no fecurity for the prefervation of Ireland, if we do not draw the bonds of our connexion much clofer, and that without delay. With fuch apprehenfions it cannot be unfeafonable to contemplate a little more clofely, the confequences of a total feparation from Ireland, and of the neceffary attendant, at leaft, in the prefent moment, on fuch a rupture, I mean her immediate alliance with the French Republic. Momentous as thefe confequences are, I fhall pafs rapidly over them, becaufe they are too obvious, and their importance too fenfible, to require, or, perhaps, admit of amplification.

An Irifh democratic republic, or rather anarchy, muft be the firft and inftant confequence of our feparation. Let any man, then, attached to the Britifh Conftitution; let any one who is

fond

fond of order and security in society, or even afraid of the extremes of disorder; let any one who would shrink from universal plunder, confiscation and murder, with all the nameless miseries, wretchedness and guilt, which are but the particulars of that aggregate called anarchy; let any man, I say, who has either the slightest concern for the human race and its happiness, a spark of love for his country, or even a common and vulgar solicitude for his own or his childrens' security, reflect for a moment on the triumphant establishment of a democratic anarchy in Ireland. It is not enough to say *" Proximus ardet;"* it is part of our own tenement which is in flames, and we come in absolute contact with this pestilent contagion. Let us, I say, consider soberly, if you please, but deeply and seriously, how much this danger would be increased by such an event, and what the nature of the danger is. I will not insist on this topic; it might lead me too far. But I shall pass to consequences of another sort.

Let us consider, for example, what would be the situation of the western coasts of this island, from the Land's-end to the Hebrides. Let us

ask

ask Cornwall, Devonshire, Bristol, Wales, Liverpool, Lancashire, Glasgow; let us ask those whose houses now stand on the margin of the Irish Channel, whose lawns and gardens are washed by that sea, which now separates them only from friends; let us ask those manufacturing coasts and counties, and those great trading cities which I have enumerated, and which now draw wealth and profit, without danger, from that channel, what their condition and that of their country will be, when they stand within hail of a powerful and savage enemy, which the darkness of a single night can bring to their chamber doors. At present the British commerce and the British navy pass freely through this channel, with friendly ports and coasts on either side, as if it were an inland navigation; while the ships of the enemy cannot approach, nor entangle themselves either for war or trade, with this maritime pass. But after such a change, when Ireland is hostile, and in the hands of an enemy, let those who direct our naval affairs, and who, I will take this opportunity of saying it, do so with so much honour to themselves, and so much solid advantage, as well as glory, to their country;

let

let thofe who are beft acquainted with our maritime fituation, declare, what new exertion of vigilance will be required, what additional number of fhips and of feamen muft be retained from offenfive war, and muft abandon the ocean, to protect the coafts of Great Britain againft thofe of Ireland, and to watch the ports of the latter country in its whole circumference. Let us reflect on the advantage loft to the Britifh navy and its operations, by exclufion from Cork, and from the fouthern and weftern harbours of Ireland; let that difadvantage be only doubled by adding our lofs to the gain of the enemy, when they have all the ports and bays of Ireland at their difpofal or in their occupation. How many fquadrons more muft we employ to tend at once the armaments of Breft and L'Orient, and thofe of Ireland. What will be the fituation of our channel and our weftern trade, when enemies' cruizers iffue from and fhelter in France to the fouthward, and Ireland to the northward, and far to the weftward of the entrance of our channel. The Victualling Board will tell us how the navy will be fupplied, when Cork is fhut againft us, and victuals only the Breft fquadrons. When the ports of Ireland are all French,

French, will it be equally impossible to transport troops from France, as when those troops were to fight their way on shore, and the ships, which transported and convoyed them were to fight their way back to France? When a French and Irish army, receiving their orders from the French Directory, are at Belfast, and ready to embark within three hours sail of the British coast, will invasion be as chimerical and visionary as it now is from France to the southern counties of England? Will in fine internal discontent, or speculative error, or the secret machinations of French corruption and English treason, or will popular hope in the first sweets of disorder and anarchy have less, or will they not have much more heart and confidence, when with the example of a successful rebellion, they have also the support of neighbouring armies to encourage them?

These are some, far from all, it would be difficult to enumerate thus suddenly all the consequences of Irish separation from Great Britain, and connexion with France, as it would affect ourselves. I am far from saying, I will never admit that even these accumulated difficulties,

difficulties, would prove too many for the hitherto unmatched powers of British energy or wifdom. But I fay the change would be great, the danger as yet untried, and the iſſue more doubtful than our prudence as Englifhmen, and much more, our duty as entruſted with the intereſts of our country, fhould permit us to expofe it to, if the trial can be averted by any honourable means. It appears to me the greateſt peril to which the Britifh Empire, whether we confider its power and greatneſs without, or its fecurity, freedom, and independence within, ever was or can be expofed. On the queſtion, therefore, as it regards Great Britain, I have no hefitation in aſſenting to the meafure, and concurring in this addreſs.

This confideration might, perhaps, be thought in ſtrictneſs fufficient for the attention of this Parliament, fince the Parliament of Ireland is no doubt competent to deliberate and decide on all that regards the intereſt of Ireland in this queſtion. No man is lefs difpofed than I am, to controvert the concurrent competence of the Irifh Parliament to deliberate, and its exclufive competence to decide

H 2 the

the queſtion as it regards Ireland. I muſt, neverthelefs, think the intereſt of Ireland in this meaſure, a very material point in the deliberation of the Britiſh Parliament alſo. For although an entire union with that country appears to be defirable on a feparate view of Britiſh intereſt; yet it would, in my opinion, ceafe to be fo, if it were not advantageous to Ireland alſo. The benefit muſt be mutual in this mutual tranfaction, in order to be enjoyed by either. The evils attending feparation would not be removed, but on the contrary would in my judgment, be much enhanced, by any meaſure which ſhould unite us at the expence, or to the effential prejudice of either. If fincere and cordial harmony is not the fruit of union; if identity in conſtitution is not founded on identity of intereſt, and is not followed by identity of fentiment and feeling towards the united empire, fuch an union will not cure the evils of imperfect relation, or even feparation, but may bring fome of them nearer and more home to both; and will produce but few of thofe advantages which I confider as the true inducements to that meaſure. I claim it, therefore, as an Engliſh queſtion, to enquire whether Union with Great Britain

will

will be beneficial to Ireland; and I should propose to pursue that enquiry not for the purpose of instructing Ireland in her own interests or duties, but for that of informing ourselves of the interest of our own country in this measure, and resting the judgment of the British Parliament, if it should be favourable to it, on the only solid and secure basis, of mutual and reciprocal advantage.

I am, therefore, to consider the consequences which would result to Ireland, from that situation of which I have already described some of the consequences to England; I mean a total separation from Great Britain, and alliance with the French Republic. I have already assumed as the first fruit of this event, or probably as either preceding or accompanying it, the abolition, in all its parts, of the present constitution of Ireland, the zealous attachment to which is opposed to all the advantages of Union, and the establishment on its ruins, of an Irish Republic on the French model. This change and all the complicated calamity it bears *in gremio*, I consider as more fatal than all the rest to the happiness of Ireland; but I will rather postpone its consideration

sideration for a moment, and advert to the other less important, indeed, but yet serious effects of such a revolution. It implies then, in the first place, a state of open hostility to England; and this warfare must in all probability partake of the nature of civil war. For it cannot be imagined, that Ireland should be unanimous in surrendering a free Government and embracing French chains; nor in preferring that abhord compound of guilt and madness, of infamy and ruin, to the blessings of religion, law, honour, security, and genuine freedom; nor is it imaginable that Ireland will be unanimous in rejecting British connexion for the purpose of fraternizing with France. The event which I have supposed, I have supposed to be the issue of war, in which one party in Ireland, now the strongest, and I trust the most numerous, has been subdued. But submission to force does not change the mind; and were such a calamity to befall Ireland, the new Irish Directory will find that the armies of England, when employed in the rescue of Ireland from that slavery, will be seconded by a great and powerful portion of their subjects. Ireland then is doomed in this event, to foreign and internal war, with all its

complicated

complicated miseries, of which the bitterness is indeed, yet on the palate of that unhappy country. I have already spoken of the disadvantages to which even England would be subjected from the hostility of Ireland. It is manifest that the country which is the least powerful on shore, and is null at sea, must labour under the same disadvantage multiplied in an infinite degree. A French army in Ireland is the natural consequence of this state of things: if that army is weak, it cannot protect them; if it is strong and adequate to the objects of France in sending it, as assuredly it will be, Ireland becomes a miserable province of France. But Ireland as a separate state, must alone provide for all the imperial establishments to which she now contributes but a part. Ireland must have an army all her own, and she will find she must subsidize her allied army, not by treaty only, but by requisition and contribution, and every other form of exaction and extortion, limited by the modesty of the French Directors, their Generals, and all their subordinate officers of plunder. They must have fortified towns, and all the establishments of that costly branch of defence. They must have a navy, build ships, maintain

arsenals

arsenals and dock-yards, supply their navy with stores and provisions, and they must man and pay their fleets, all from their own funds and resources. Have the œconomists of Ireland computed the price of these imperial honours, if indeed, they can be borne at all? But let them consider, whether the insulated trade and wealth of Ireland will furnish either men or money for such demands, even after the people should have so far belied all the experience which the world has had of them, by submitting with perfect obedience to the utmost exactions that can be laid upon them. It would after all be worthy of a moment's reflexion, whether if Ireland should not suddenly accomplish that which France, Spain, and Holland, seconded by an armed neutrality of the maritime powers of the North; that is to say, what the whole naval world have tried in vain, I mean should not suddenly acquire a superiority at sea over Great Britain, whether her commerce and every hope which her insular situation could suggest or realize, must not be held by sufferance, and at the mercy of that powerful and offended neighbour, to whom nature had allied her, but whose generous offer of an equal and honourable participation

pation in power, profperity and happinefs fhe had rejected with infult, as if it had been an injury. Ireland will, no doubt, not expect after her feparation from England, and alliance with our enemies, to partake freely in our Eaft India or our colonial trade; nor will fhe expect of England in thofe circumftances, the great and liberal facrifices which fhe now makes to the fupport and promotion of Irifh induftry, with the amount and particulars of which a noble Lord has juft made us acquainted; facrifices which, however liberal in their extent, and however beneficial to Ireland in their effect, I confider only as a natural indulgence of fraternal affection, as well as a wife exertion of imperial policy, while we are united; but which muft of neceffity expire with our connexion. Will the trade of France, or the fhare of it to which they would be admitted, and the conditions of its tenure, compenfate this lofs? Will reftraints and prohibitions on the commercial intercourfe between England and Ireland be no lofs to the latter country? The papers on your Lordfhips' table will inftruct us on that point.

The considerations which I have already enumerated are of no light or trivial import; but I must now set before the eyes of Irish gentlemen, one inseparable consequence of such a revolution, and one of which they are no doubt aware. I mean the expulsion and confiscation, not to say the blood of those who now support their antient connexion with England; and whom the case I have stated supposes to have been defeated. But will confiscation and murder go no deeper even than this? In the savage triumph of democratical anarchy, will not every friend to the established constitution of Ireland, to the authority of law, or even to the moral restraints of virtue and religion, will not every one who is guilty of that unpardonable irremissible crime, the possession of property, real or personal, great or small, will not in a word all those whose situation seems to offer either a lure, or a curb to violence, be involved in that undistinguishing massacre and pillage which sweeps the way before and bears up the train of such revolutions? I must indeed put it, my Lords, seriously and earnestly, not as a topic of declamation, or false and artificial feeling, but as furnishing

nishing the soundest argument, and exciting the warmest solicitude, to the property, and I may say to the industry, and to the virtue of Ireland, without distinction of degree, or of religious persuasion, what would be the consequence of a complete victory obtained by France in Ireland, what would be the inevitable consequence of delivering Ireland, with all her political, religious and civil interests, over to the discretion of that description of Irishmen who would then become their masters, and of that description of anarchy which must follow such events as I have described.---I choose rather to hint at than to dwell on such topics. They are indeed fitter for the private meditation of those who are concerned in them, than for a public discussion or rhetorical amplification. I am content with having stated shortly and dispassionately the nature and degree of some of those dangers which may induce England to consent to Union, but which seem to command Ireland, with the authority of urgent and instant necessity, to seek without delay, the refuge which this measure presents to her.

It is impossible to overlook some circumstances in the internal and political condition of Ireland, which bear as powerfully on the question of Union, and seem to recommend that measure to the people of Ireland, as strongly for the purposes of equal government, and of civil and municipal happiness, as on any other grounds whatever. Ireland is a divided country, but unequally divided as to property and numbers; the least numerous class possessing the property and the power; but the most numerous entertaining, and indeed cherishing fondly, and tenaciously, claims on both, I mean both on the property and the power. I need not detain your Lordships by describing the extent or the violence of those passions which inflame and exasperate both parts of the Irish nation against each other. Every one knows the firm and immoveable basis on which their mutual hatred stands, the irreconcileable nature of its motives, its bitter, malignant, and implacable character. In this frame and temper of mind, however, towards each other, one of these portions of Ireland claims and exercises what is felt by both, to be a species of dominion over the other.

other. I believe it is hardly too much to say, that there are two nations in Ireland; two Irish peoples; the one sovereign, the other subject. The sovereign class, or cast of Irishmen, claim their sovereignty as of right, and ground it on an old title of conquest, confirmed, as they contend, by possession, acquiescence, and prescription. They claim also the federal support of Great Britain in maintaining this dominion, on the solemn grounds of fidelity to implied compact, compensation for sacrifices, and reward for services. They shew a close alliance and identity of views between themselves and the English interest in Ireland in all times, and they rely as strongly on recent, and even on present exertions in a common cause, as on the uniform tenour of their ancient services. In a word, they call at once upon our honour and our gratitude, and they support that appeal by a stream and series of facts which we cannot controvert. I must confess that I have always felt this point as constituting a true and proper dilemma—on the one hand, I cannot admit the ascendancy of one part of a nation, over another part of the same nation, to the extent and to the purpose claimed in Ireland, as capable of assuming any character deserving the denomination of right. That which is a wrong on one side, cannot, intelligibly to me, become a right in the other. Wrong is not a material out of which it appears possible to construct right; and I do not think the virtues of possession, prescription, or any other limitation of time, which are supposed to cure the vices of a bad title, at all applicable to the case of perpetually subsisting, and, as it were, renovating wrongs, especially such as affect the political rights of great numbers of men. The operation of prescription in confirming titles, even in the private transactions of property, is, indeed, different, I believe, from the common notion that is formed of it. Prescription does not cure the original vice of a bad title; but, after all memory of the good title, which had been supplanted by the usurped one, has been lost and buried under the oblivion of time, prescription, that is to say, the lapse of time within which legal memory can survive, determines the expiration of the old title and gives effect, not to the bad one which first superseded it, but to a new title arising out of possession, and consummated in this manner by the completion of prescriptive time.

Nothing of this applies to subsisting and continuing wrongs, in which the length of their duration, and the frequency of their repetition, instead of diminishing the injury, must be felt to be a grievous aggravation, and instead of converting wrong into right, seems only to improve and fortify the title of those who suffer, to shake off the injury on the first opportunity that offers. If possession then will not constitute this singular right which is claimed in wrong, as between the parties themselves, neither can it be improved by the interests, the engagements, or the obligations of a third party: and I do not see how the *jus tertii*, as it may be called, of England, can affect the relative claims of these two Irish nations, or of these two parts of the Irish nation. On this ground, therefore, and merely on this general and abstract view of the question, I confess I might have thought it difficult to assign a sufficient reason to preclude his Majesty as Sovereign of Ireland, from concurring with his Irish Parliament, or even from exerting, in every lawful way, his legitimate powers in promoting such measures as might be calculated to place every class of his Irish subjects on an equal footing, as to civil rights, and confolidate thefe two hoftile nations into one peaceable and united family.—But in truth your Lordfhips know that nothing can be lefs rational, nor more dangerous, and often fatal than thefe abftract views of practical queftions, affecting the interefts of multitudes and of nations. In the blind purfuit of abftract right, we fhall often find ourfelves, innocently no doubt, if our intention be confidered, but yet too effectually, the inftruments of great practical injuftice and oppreffion. I believe there are few cafes to which this obfervation applies more clofely, than to that which we are confidering.—That part of Ireland which we would wifh to redrefs, claim not only political equality in the Government of their country, a claim in which I confefs I cannot help fympathifing with them; but they are known to entertain, and to nourifh yet more fondly and anxioufly, though perhaps not yet fo loudly or diftinctly pronounced, claims of a very different nature. We cannot be ignorant that the firft application of thofe rights with which we fhould be difpofed to inveft them, is likely to be the perpetration of a great wrong, and that at bottom, that wrong was, perhaps, the true and eventual object of their actual demand, and would be the practical result of its attainment. The Catholics of Ireland not only claim a participation in the civil franchises enjoyed by their Protestant countrymen; but they foster claims on the *property* of Protestants, the present possession of which they treat as mere usurpation, and these claims are of no trifling extent. We know the aspiring character of their church, or if you please, of all churches, or of all bodies and descriptions of men. We must, above all, recollect what is perhaps more urgent than all the rest, that the Catholics, besides their claims, civil or religious, have passions to gratify, passions long irritated, long restrained, but not on that account the less vehement, or dangerous. I have heard such apprehensions treated lightly, as the productions either of imagination or ignorance; and I certainly pretend to no credit on such points, from personal knowledge or inquiry. I should wish therefore to qualify any thing that may appear rash or peremptory, in what I hazard on such a subject, by avowing that degree of diffidence in my own views, which may be thought becoming with regard to facts, which though attested, I think, satisfactorily by others, have

not

not fallen under my own observation. But with this qualification, I confess that I find it difficult to resist a conclusion to which the general knowledge we may all possess of the human character, applied to such facts as all admit, seems to lead us. I must therefore profess a strong impression, that if to the physical force already possessed by the Catholic body, and which consists in superiority of numbers, were added by any such revolution as that which we are considering, the advantages of political power, and the weight and influence which belong to the authority of Government and Legislation, some danger might accrue to the property, the establishment, and even the personal security of the Protestant in Ireland; and with this apprehension on our own minds, the alarm expressed by those who are so deeply interested in the consequences of such measures, seems entitled to our serious and earnest attention.

I am not more clear, therefore, in thinking the Catholics entitled to a fair participation in the civil and political franchises of Irishmen, than I am in feeling, that the Protestants ought

to

to be protected and defended in the security of their property, their religion, and their persons, against every violence which the Catholics might be disposed to attempt, when they have passed from their present state of subjection to that of authority and power. The dilemma, therefore, has hitherto consisted in this. The Protestants could not be supported in that ascendancy which seems necessary even for their protection, without derogating from what may appear to be a natural right of the Catholics. The Catholics could not be supported in their claim of equality, without transferring to them that ascendancy which equality of rights must draw to the larger body, and which from that moment must expose the Protestants to dangers from which they ought to be protected. Such seem to be the practical difficulties in the way of abstract justice, while the Government of Ireland continues merely local. An Irish Parliament, in which the ascendancy is either Protestant or Catholic, and it cannot choose, but lie on one side or the other, may be expected still, I fear, to gore and lacerate their country, by one or other of the horns of this dilemma; and I see no perfect remedy for Irish division, and its lamentable confequences, while thefe two enraged and implacable opponents are ftill fhut up together, are ftill enclofed within the very theatre, on the very arena of their ancient and furious contention. I do fincerely think that this divided and double condition of the Irifh people requires fomething of an *imperial aula,* a legiflature founded on a broader and more liberal bafis, to adminifter impartial laws to all, and to reconcile fecurity with juftice. While one of thefe parties muft judge the other, in which ever hand the fafces may be placed, I fear there is reafon to expect only violence in the fuit, and if not injuftice, at leaft flow and imperfect juftice in the decree. My mind, I confefs, cannot refift the conviction arifing out of all thefe confiderations, that the united Parliament of Great Britain and Ireland, will in the peculiar circumftances of Ireland, conftitute a better legiflature, and a more perfect, becaufe a more impartial Parliament, for all Ireland, than any reprefentation of a minor part or fection of Ireland, in a feparate, local Parliament ever can. I am perfuaded that laws beneficial to the mafs of the people of Ireland, and promoting its general profperity and happiness, may be expected with greater confidence from the united Parliament, in which local partialities, interests, and passions, will not divert the straight and equal current of legislation, than in an Irish Parliament, where these stumbling blocks must for ever bend or impede its course. In the united Parliament right may be done unaccompanied by wrong. Irish Catholics may be invested with their political capacities, without the slightest danger to Protestant establishment or property. These, on the contrary, must acquire a tenfold and hundredfold security in the Protestant Parliament, and the genuine Protestant ascendancy of the united kingdom—The Protestant church and property may, on the other hand, be secured, without perpetuating the present humiliating and degrading exclusion of the Catholic part of the Irish nation. Such are some of the particularities in the condition of Ireland, which appear to me to add in her case, many powerful inducements to those which in every other instance may invite neighbouring and friendly countries to a close and intimate union of their governments.

I con-

I confess, that to me these considerations furnish, by no means the weakest recommendation of this measure. I look with peculiar satisfaction towards the prospect which it seems to open, I think in truth, for the first time in the history of Ireland, of doing justice to one part of that nation without injury to the other, and of providing for the general prosperity and happiness, without bringing calamity on any particular part. For I cannot consider the admission of fellow citizens to a participation of common franchises, as an injury to those who happen already to possess them; nor the loss or even destitution of partial and exclusive dominion over fellow subjects, as any wrong. The Protestants have a sacred right to their properties, to their religion and to their own liberties; but the liberties of their Catholic brethren are no part of that property; they have no narrow corporate right, or none that I can wish to support them in, in the government of their countrymen; nor can I see that the subjection of the Catholics must be an article in the charter of Protestant liberties.

If

If the Union, therefore, present a hope of meliorating the condition, and extinguishing the discontents of a great majority of the inhabitants of Ireland, without exposing the rest to danger, but on the contrary, adding the most substantial securities to all their legitimate rights, I must profess myself on that account, and perhaps, I may say, principally on that account, a warm friend to the measure; and I am free to confess that if these were not to be the consequences, I should expect very little advantage from it. I am desirous, therefore, of declaring for myself, that I shall think the Union much more perfect, much better adapted to all its beneficial ends, and the benefits to be expected from it, in such a case, I think incalculable, if the just claims of the Catholic Irish are provided for by an explicit article of the treaty itself. After having thus declared my own mind, and distinctly pronounced my own judgment on this great leading point, I think it right to add, that if any political peculiarities of the present time, should render it impracticable to engross these wholesome provisions in the written treaty itself, I would rather restrain my wishes for the

imme-

immediate accomplishment of this desirable end, than expose this great transaction to needless and unprofitable hazard, by unseasonable pertinacity or impatience. And I should still look with confidence to a period when the object I have mentioned will result as a natural consequence, from the treaty, and when this desirable change will flow, with many other blessings, from the impartiality of the imperial and united legislature—If I were worthy then of offering to the loyal Catholics of Ireland the advice of an individual, who has no other claim to their attention, than that of uniting a spirit of liberal toleration, and a strong favour towards common right as opposed to monopoly, of combining, I say, these sentiments with something of a practicable disposition which would not reject attainable good when a more perfect accomplishment of right is out of reach, I would implore their prudent acquiescence in a measure which must ultimately consolidate their interests with those of their country; which will bring, in its season, relief to the Catholics and security to the Protestants of Ireland; which will improve the wealth, the

prosperity,

prosperity, the dignity, the manners, and the public and private happiness of their country; and which conferring these blessings with one hand, will avert with the other, the certain ruin, desolation and slavery, which are at this moment impending over their native land.

I wish to guard against one misinterpretation. When I prefer the United Parliament to that of Ireland, as at present constituted, I should be much misunderstood, if I were thought to profess a distrust of the wisdom and justice of the Irish Parliament in general, or to impute to it the slightest degree of incompetence to the general objects of its legislative duties. I profess, on the contrary, the highest and most unfeigned respect, both for the Irish Parliament as a body, and for many of its members, with whom I have, indeed, little, or I might nearly say, no personal acquaintance, but whose characters and talents, as public men, I have contemplated, as others do, with the respect and admiration they justly inspire. What I have hazarded on this subject, the delicacy of which I am not insensible to, amounts only to this; that in one great branch and member of Irish affairs, the present

sent Irish Parliament must be considered as a party, and in those concerns, a major part of the people must now receive the law from an adverse and rival authority. Whereas, in the United Parliament, the Irish members will furnish all the local information, and will possess all the weight and influence, which the general affairs and interests of that country require; while those local or partial feelings which might warp the judgment of the best intentioned Irishmen, on some subjects, might be moderated, and temperated, by the mediating impartiality of the imperial Parliament.

I would now consider one or two general objections, which I have observed to be most prominent in the opposition to this measure, and I shall begin with that which appears to have been the most operative and successful throughout Ireland, and to have had the greatest share in the rejection of this important and salutary proposal. I mean the notion, that a Legislative Union, however beneficial in its effect, to the interests of Ireland, is, however, in some way, derogatory to the honour, and national independance of that country.

The

The whole of this topic will be found to be an appeal from reason to feeling, and, indeed, from a just and genuine feeling to a blind and inconsiderate one. It is intended, like most of the objections on this question, to preclude the discussion of its merits; and what is peculiar to this particular objection, it is not only intended to elude the merits of the principal question, but seems to disclaim the discussion even of any proper and specific merits of its own. It is used, in truth, to disqualify those to whom it is presented for all deliberation whatever, by exciting the passions, and interposing the flame and dazzle of enthusiasm, between the eye and the object it is to examine. Those who employ this topic, have undoubtedly a considerable advantage; for, in the first place, many more are susceptible of strong and lively feeling, than capable, or willing, to form an enlightened and deliberate judgment on any subject whatever. In the next place, the feeling applied to, is in itself by no means unnatural, and so far from being culpable, or a subject of reproach, must, on the contrary, be classed with those affections which are the most beneficial to the world,

and

and the moſt honourable to thoſe who poſſeſs them. It is, in a word, a branch or mode of patriotiſm, that virtue which embraces the whole range of our public duties, and which is an object of too much reſpect and veneration, when genuine and well directed, not to challange ſome indulgence even in its errors and deluſions. I cannot, however, help ſuſpecting, that thoſe who avoid diſcuſſion, are not very firm or confident on the merits; and that paſſion is ſeldom excluſively applied to, when reaſon is on the ſame ſide. Enthuſiaſm is, indeed, in general, to be accounted but an unſafe and unfaithful guide. The guide is himſelf blind, and I know not how to ſearch for truth with better hope of ſucceſs, than by the light of ſuch reaſon as Providence may have beſtowed upon us. I ſhould propoſe, therefore, to follow that courſe, and to conſider diſpaſſionately, even this paſſion. I would fairly and deliberately enquire, whether a ſincere regard for the national dignity of Ireland, does, indeed, oppoſe any ſolid objection to a Legiſlative Union with Great Britain.

I ſhall

I shall waste but little of your Lordships' time, in analyzing the nature and foundation of those local affections towards particular spots, which seem to circumscribe the general benevolence of mankind within the rivers or seas, or mountains, which encompass that which we call our country. Perhaps that expansive love of our fellow creatures, which has obtained the general name of philanthropy, may have been compressed into narrower bounds, in order to augment its energy in the proper scene of its exertion; perhaps this large and diffuse motive may have been drawn home as it were, and retrenched within limits more commensurate with the size and sphere of human action. But no matter how or why, the love of our country certainly exists; it is the noblest affection of the human breast; and I have no doubt is of divine origin—I am to acknowledge that Ireland, both by its dimensions, its local position, and every other circumstance attending it, offers a fit object for that passion, the ardour of which may well be improved into enthusiasm and zeal, by the many natural charms which, I understand, abound in that country, and by that to which

I can,

I can, indeed, speak myself, I mean the many generous qualities which distinguish its inhabitants, and seem to endear that nation to those who compose it—I am willing also to admit, that besides that solicitude for the happiness and well-being of the people who inhabit our country, which is the proper and distinctive feature by which true patriotism is to be recognized, this local affection may also attach a sort of interest, and a certain importance and value, to the separate political existence, or individuality, of that country. That identical space has contained the habitual objects of our regard, and an association may have been established between our local and moral attachment, in such a manner as to render it, perhaps, no easy abstraction, to love the people of Ireland, distinctly from that which may be called the love of Ireland. Nothing of all this need be controverted; nor is it desirable that it should be otherwise—I would only demand a similar assent to some particularities, which I think observable in this passion, and which appear to me to bear, in some degree, on the principal question. This local patriotism, then, seems to be limited ed not only by space, as we have seen, but also with some reference to time. The space to which the affection of patriotism attaches, is that which we have been accustomed to consider as our country, at a given time, that is to say, in our own time, or during our own generation. If it had been larger or smaller at our birth, our love would have expanded or contrrcted itself accordingly. We have seen a remarkable instance of this expansive property in local patriotism, or in this love of metes and bounds, as related by Mr. Hume, in the passage which I have read from his history of the Union of the Heptarchy. We have seen in that example, the inhabitants of the six conquered kingdoms transfer their allegiance to Egbert, and the minute partialities of these six countries, transgress their respective bounds, and in obedience to events, dilate, as by common consent, so as to occupy the whole surface of the united kingdom of England, and accommodate themselves to this change of boundary, with as much rapidity and ease, as the ambition of the Monarch himself had done to the growth of his dominions. This happened in the very season of

repug-

repugnance and difguft which fucceeds to conqueft, and a vanquifhed Mercian or Eaft Angle, ceafed even in his own life, to think himfelf degraded by being called an Englifhman.

The fame truth has been evinced in Wales. Thofe who inhabited that principality in the early part of the reign of Harry the 8th, felt their patriotifm and national feelings bounded by the mountains of their country, beyond which, indeed, fo far from difcovering the objects of affection, they found only thofe of antient animofity and habitual hoftility. The fame narrow bounds, however, no longer limit the public fpirit and affections of thofe who have inhabited that part of our ifland fince that memorable and fortunate æra in the hiftory of Wales. I believe I may venture to fay, that none of your Lordfhips who may have an intereft in that country, and that no Welch gentleman, or inhabitant of Wales, would thank a Welch patriot who fhould propofe to reftore the dignity and independence of that country, by feparating it once more from England; that is to fay, who

fhould

should forbid and prohibit every Welchman, from presuming to consider himself as entitled to any participation in the affairs, in the enterprizes, in the greatness, consideration, or glory of that empire, of which his country is now a distinguished member. They would, no doubt, think the dignity of their countrymen strangely provided for by this second extermination; by driving them once more out of England, and cooping them up within the mountains of Wales, as the Saxon Conquerors had done by their British ancestors. I shall not easily persuade myself, that a Welch gentleman will think an affront or indignity is put upon himself, or his country, because Lord NELSON, for example, can take him by the hand as fellow-subject; or because his countryman *FOLEY was enabled, by the union of Wales, to lead the British fleet into action on the 1st of August, instead of heading some miserable predatory inroad across the Welch marches.

I may speak with better authority of another country. Those who inhabited Scotland in the reign of King William; those who

* Captain Foley, of his Majesty's ship Goliah.

inhabited that part of Scotland with which I am beſt acquainted, and who looked from their windows on the hills of Northumberland, at a few miles diſtance, had their patriotiſm bounded by their horizon, or rather their eye had a wider range than this large and liberal paſſion. It is not ſo with thoſe who inhabit that country in the reign of George the Third, and this change, I am perſuaded, was operated much ſooner than ſome Noble Lords ſeem diſpoſed to allow. A Noble Lord, (Lord Holland,) referred, on a former occaſion, to a proceeding of this Houſe in the year 1713, as furniſhing ſome ground to ſuppoſe that the two countries were not ſoon reconciled to the Union. I am by no means diſpoſed to deny, that the tranſaction alluded to, might furniſh a very fair argument to be uſed in debate on this topic. It certainly imported, in its literal acceptation, the wiſh, at leaſt of ſome individuals, for a diſſolution of the Union, being an expreſs motion for that purpoſe. It was negatived, indeed, by the Houſe; but it was made by one of the ſixteen Scotch Peers, and ſupported, generally, though I do not know that it was unanimouſly, by that body. I have no reason to complain, therefore, of this proceeding being used in argument, to the point for which it was adduced; but I must say, at the same time, that it does not appear to me as conclusive, as I am to presume it did to that Noble Lord. Your Lordships' leisure will not admit of my entering minutely into all the particulars of this proceeding; but I must at least say, that it has by no means made the same impression on my mind, and I am not satisfied, that the people of Scotland or of England, or the Peerage of Scotland at large, or their representatives in this House who supported this motion, including even the mover of the question himself, were in earnest in desiring the separation of the united kingdoms. I do not think myself bound to believe, merely on the letter of a motion in Parliament, any body of men, and especially that enlightened body to which I allude, capable of harbouring a design so absurd, and if sincere, so wicked and detestable, as that motion imported, while I can find any other motive, or can imagine any other object more rational and less culpable, to account sufficiently for the proceeding. I find then, no difficulty in difcovering abundant inducements for this motion, short of the absurd and incredible purpose which it expresses—I observe, in the first place, that it was made in the House of Lords, and originated with the sixteen Peers of Scotland. The Scotch Peerage was undoubtedly the body whose interests were least consulted, and who were the worst treated by the Union. But they had received fresh cause of complaint subsequent to that event. The abolition of the Privy Council of Scotland was, in my opinion, necessary to consolidate the Union, by removing that remaining nucleus of a local government, and separate interest. But this measure affected, no doubt, the views both of ambition and of vanity, of the Scotch Peerage and of the higher order of the gentry, though it very little concerned the people. The discontent of the Peerage excited by that measure, had been yet more recently enflamed by the decision of this House in the case of the Duke of Hamilton. His patent, as Duke of Brandon, had been disallowed, and by that proceeding it seemed decided, that a Scotch Peer, after the Union, should be incapable of receiving the independent dignity of a British Peerage;

Peerage; a difability highly injurious to the Peerage of Scotland, in its fondeft aim, and reafonably offenfive and difgufting to that body, already fore with prior provocations. If we confider this motion, then, as no more than the expreffion of the chagrin of this body; but efpecially if it be confidered as a means employed to give weight in future to their juft pretenfions, we fhall affign as weighty a motive for fuch a proceeding as has produced many others of great importance in Parliament. Thefe grievances were, indeed, exprefsly ftated in the motion, amongft the reafons on which it was grounded. But the fpecial occafion of this tranfaction was the extenfion of the malt-tax to Scotland. This tax was, in fact, felt to be oppreffive on that country, and it was, befides, fairly queftionable whether the impofition of this tax at that particular point of time was not contrary to an article of the Union. This objection applied indeed only to that particular period, and ceafed afterwards, but it was fubject to queftion at the time. I think on the whole that the Scotch members of both Houfes were juftified in ftanding out on this tax, and I think their Union and exertion on that occa-

fion

fion did them honour, though I do not think the mode of oppofition they chofe judicious. I find, however, in the very occafion which gave rife to this proceeding, a fufficient motive, and a much more natural and indeed juftifiable purpofe than that which the motion literally imported. It was intended to enforce the oppofition of Scotland to the malt-tax, and to coerce the Minifter on that point, not by the diffolution of the Union, but by the intimidation which the very menace of fuch a fatal ftep might be expected to produce. The Englifh Peers who fupported this motion had themfelves been the authors and promoters of the Union. But they were the oppofition of the day, and it appears, could not deny themfelves the fatisfaction of ufing the opportunity which this Scotch queftion of the malt-tax afforded them, of diftreffing the Minifter of the day, by the fingular and rare union of the Reprefentatives of Scotland, even for a few hours, againft the Court. It lafted, indeed, no longer; and the oppofition of the fixteen Peers feems to have fpent and exhaufted itfelf in this fingle act, in which I can difcern only a general expreffion of their own particular difguft, and a wifh to ftand well

with

with their country by opposing the malt-tax. The opposition to that tax, and the attempt at least to modify it, as to Scotland, was the true occasion of this motion, and instead of so absurd and flagitious, but so important and momentous a design as that of dissolving the Union, there appears to me to have been nothing deeper in the matter, than the wish on one hand to tease a Minister, and on the other to obtain the reduction of threepence on the bushel of malt, in a tax upon Scotland. I am a good deal confirmed in this view of the transaction, by observing that although this tax was renewed every year, and was objected to by the Scotch members in the House of Commons, I do not find a hint of any new intention to dissolve the Union. Various other questions interesting to Scotland were discussed, without producing the slightest intimation of such a design; and I find one, very little posterior to that on which the noble Lord has relied, so remarkable, that I cannot help mentioning it; I mean the extraordinary bill, known by the name of the Peerage Bill, which actually passed this House in the year 1719, but was thrown out, as might be expected, in the House of Commons.

Neither

Neither the Peerage of Scotland, nor the Scotch nation, have ever received, fince the Union, fo fignal a provocation as that bill appears to me to have offered to them. It propofed, in direct terms, the complete disfranchifement of the whole body of the Scotch Peers, and ftripped them even of the elective franchife which the Union had left them, without any other compenfation worthy of notice, than that of feeing fuch of their reprefentatives as were parties to this fpoliation, rewarded by Britifh Peerages, which were to make them independent in future, of the favour, or refentment of their injured conftituents. This meafure, as your Lordfhips muft fee, was, at the fame time, the moft flagrant violation of the Union in fome of its moft fundamental articles, and could not fail of exciting general difguft and alarm throughout Scotland, by breaking fo wantonly the integrity, and fhaking the fecurity of that folemn treaty. The Bill was accordingly debated with great warmth, at great length, and, I think, with much ability in both Houfes of Parliament; and I have troubled your Lordfhips with thefe particulars, for the purpofe of obferving, that throughout thofe debates, on a fubject fufficiently

ently offensive and irritating to Scotland, there was not dropped from the lips of a single individual, an intimation of any such wish for separation, as had been expressed in the proceeding of the year 1713. A certain proof that such a wish could not be general in either country, and a pretty conclusive argument that it was not professed or entertained by any considerable party or description of men then known in England or Scotland. On this review of the period immediately succeeding the Union, I might, without much prejudice to my argument, concede all the Noble Lord can claim from the motion of 1713, though I am far from making that admission in fact; but if I were to grant that in the year 1713, some indications of indisposition and alienation between the countries remained; that six short years of Union had not completely appeased and obliterated the animosities of four centuries, but that six years more had been sufficient for that purpose; that after the lapse of six years from their Union, no trace of unkindness was discernible, and, that in twelve years after that Union, the strongest provocation had failed in exciting it, I do not think, I say, that for the purpose of the present argument, I shall

shall have made a conceffion of much value or importance; and with this remark I shall pass forward to times of which I am entitled to speak with the confidence of perfonal knowledge. I will venture then to affure your Lordships, and to speak for my neighbours as well as myfelf, that at this day we fee without humiliation or regret, thofe towers and beacons, which were very neceffary appendages of our independence, at leaft, before the union of the crowns; when we had a predatory enemy within ten miles of us; we behold, I fay, without mortification or concern, thofe badges of imperial dignity mouldering, and in ruins, on our rocks, while we can fee the plains below covered with crops, which he who fows is now fure of reaping; and while we can extend our views of national greatnefs and dignity, and all our public feelings, whether of pride or of affection, not only beyond the little range of hills that we look upon, but to the remoteft extremities of the habitable globe. I will venture to declare for my country, that with the exception of thofe falfe Scotchmen, whom the enemy has been able to corrupt or to delude, and who, I truft, for the honour of Scotland, are both few and contemptible; but with that

exception

exception of the partizans of France, I will venture to pronounce, that there does not at this hour live a Scotchman of any degree or condition, from Berwick to the Orkneys, whose British patriotism would not be more offended, and certainly much more reasonably, by a proposal for separating these kingdoms, than the patriotism of Fletcher of Saltown, or Lockhart of Carnwath, could be at the beginning of the century, by the proposal for uniting them.

I have dwelt somewhat longer on this topic than, perhaps, I ought, principally for the purpose of shewing what the nature and value of that object is, for which Ireland has been persuaded to renounce and reject with anger, the greatest and most evident advantages that were ever offered to a nation. It is in the first place, then, a sentiment, or feeling, which it is difficult to define, and not perhaps easy even to conceive distinctly. In the next place, this sentiment, such as it is, is so limited in duration, and so obsequious to events, that it is not enough to say that it expires. It actually changes sides—and the very sacrifices we would make to it at one period, will, at a subsequent

sequent point of time, and from thence ever after, prove as much in contradiction with, and as offensive to, this very feeling, as it might be welcome and grateful to it before. What then is this mighty object to which such sacrifices are required? It is an airy unsubstantial sentiment; it is a transient, evanescent, metaphysical point, to which we are called upon to sacrifice not only the solid and substantial, but the permanent and perpetual interests of two great nations.

I confess I cannot persuade myself to rank a sentiment so subtle, and subject to so many refined and delicate modifications, with that sound and genuine affection, or I can class it only as a subordinate mode of that plain and manly passion, which has deserved, by excellence, the style and dignity of patriotism. True patriotism will, I think, be found to rest on the solid basis of some rational and useful principle, which will keep it uniform and uninfluenced by time or circumstance, and which may serve as a criterion to distinguish its own genuine and steady course, from the capricious and irregular motions of some of its many counterfeits. The love of our country may be

rational

rational or fantaſtical as that of any other object; and, I muſt conſider patriotiſm as partaking ſufficiently of the nature of general affection, to acknowledge it for genuine, only when it is evinced by ſolicitude for the welfare of its object. I fix on this as the diſtinctive character of ſincere affection, whether for our country or for any other object of regard. Public love is founded in utility, and by that mark alone may challenge its deſcent from Heaven. The reſt is all ſpurious, and to be viewed rather with caution than reſpect. On this clear principle, then, ſhall we not ſay, that a true patriot propoſes to himſelf before all things, the proſperity and happineſs of thoſe who inhabit his country? He may ſet a value, if he pleaſes, on the diſtinct exiſtence, and individuality of that country; but if his love be well regulated, and all its modes and affections be in due ſubordination, he will prefer the ſolid and real happineſs of his country to its metaphyſical identity. It is to this chaſte and diſciplined patriotiſm, that I would appeal, on the preſent queſtion, againſt the noiſy and clamorous pretence, which would uſurp its ſeat, and bear away the deciſion by acclamation and tumult, before a ſober and enlightened judgment,

founded

founded on the solid basis of public utility, can silence this importunate and delusive feeling. To sum up my argument on this point, in plain, but I think, satisfactory terms; if a separate political existence is contrary, nay fatal to the real interests of the people of Ireland; and if a perfect incorporation and union with the British Empire, must be productive of security, aggrandizement and happiness to Ireland, such an Union should on this single but decisive ground, of great and permanent utility, be the first and fondest wish of every Irish heart.

But let us yield even this principle for a moment. Let us subscribe to that strange incomprehensible duty which I have heard proclaimed with a sort of triumph, even in this House, and by which it is required that in a question such as this, the Legislature should banish from their thoughts and contemplation every concern for the interests of the nations which they represent, and that the decision of this mighty question should be founded on any thing but its influence on the national advantage or security. Let us admit the insignificance of Irish prosperity and happiness, and the exclusive title of what is called distinctness and dignity, to

our

our solicitude; I still say that even these objects are not provided for, by rejecting the present measure. For the choice does not lie between the present condition of Ireland and Union. We are not ignorant that the alternative is according to every moral probability, union or separation ; that is to say union or ruin; union with Great Britain, or slavery to France. If this measure be not adopted, we know that the distinctness of Ireland must expire; that her political extinction must be accomplished; that she must undergo a change a thousand fold more degrading, as well as destructive, and more fatal to her independence and dignity, by means which no mistaken patriotism can prefer. I mean by subjection to a foreign conqueror, or at best by a debased and slavish dependence on the general tyrant and task-master of Europe. Instead of preserving her present independence, or acquiring new accession of importance and dignity, by her association with the British Empire, Ireland is in danger of dropping into that common sepulchre of nations, which has already buried the very names and memories of so many states and kingdoms, now no more. Will the identity or the dignity of Ireland be
preserved,

preserved, when after being first the dupe and the servile tool of France, she becomes her real and effectual slave, under some ridiculous or antiquated nick-name, invented or revived, for the very purpose of obliterating her own?

Let us consider this question in one view more, and setting aside both the real interests of Ireland, and the chances of separation with its attendant calamities, let us only compare the present condition of Ireland in mere dignity, with its future condition, in that single respect, after the Union; for we shall find the opposers of the Union mistaken in the means of consulting even barren dignity, when they prefer the present situation of Ireland to its incorporation with the British Empire.

In what does the dignity of a nation truly consist? Is it merely in its *separate*, or in its *independent* existence? If Ireland, from the very nature of things, is, and always must, while it is a separate kingdom, remain, in some respects and in some degree, dependent, subordinate, inferior; and the day after its Union with Great Britain, becomes altogether independent, sovereign and equal, how is its dignity

nity better assured by the former condition than by the latter? We must enquire then what the present situation of Ireland truly is, in point of independence

Although I should wish to be perfectly frank and explicit, in pointing out those circumstances of necessary and unavoidable subordination which really exist, I would by no means insist on others, which I have heard enlarged upon, I think, with a false pride on our part, and perhaps with reasonable offence to the national feeling of Irishmen, and which, at the same time, do not appear to me genuine tokens of subordination in any respect. Of this description, I consider the necessity under which Ireland labours of claiming, in times of danger, whether from foreign or domestic enemies, the protection of the British navy, and military, as well as pecuniary aid from this country. I conceive Ireland to have a perfect right to this friendly and brotherly co-operation, on two grounds, which seem to me to preclude altogether, either a mortifying humiliation on one hand, or an offensive pride on the other. First, the preservation of Ireland is an English interest, and is a concern suffici-

O ently

ently precious to call for these exertions, even on a distinct and separate view of our own advantage. In the next place, Ireland is entitled to this support, from an Empire to which she is associated, and to the general service and security of which she is herself contributing, cheerfully, and at all times, in every branch of public service. Her seamen, her soldiers, and her revenue, all augment the general stock of British resources. And if peculiar and temporary emergencies have, at this, or any other particular period, encreased the local demands of Ireland on the exertions of the Empire, we must recollect, that the scene of danger, may at other times be shifted; and we have no reason to doubt, but, on the contrary, have recent grounds, very honourable to Ireland, for believing, that she will be ready to furnish extraordinary exertion, and aid, to repel extraordinary danger on this side of the water, if such occasions should arise.

I must also dissent from another topic which I have heard used, as indicating a national dependence of Ireland on Great Britain. I mean the advantages which she derives from the extensive commerce without, and the prosperous

manu-

manufactures within, which are supposed to flow, and which, I believe, really do flow, in a great part, from a free participation in the imperial greatness of Great Britain, and from encouragements which she might withhold if so advised. Here again, I think, Ireland may accept, I will not say, without gratitude, but without humiliation, as Great Britain ought to bestow without pride. When the question has been stated between entire separation and Union, these considerations are very pertinently submitted to the prudence of Ireland, as they have been, with great ability, by the Noble Lord * who preceded me; for the advantages alluded to, would, no doubt, be withdrawn with perfect justice, and indeed, by indispensible policy, if all connexion between us were dissolved. But when the question is placed on the footing of the present argument, that is to say, on a view of our present imperial relation, I then feel, that considering the importance of that relation to Great Britain, as well as to Ireland, the communication of these imperial advantages seems to belong to the very nature of the case, and to flow naturally from the

* Lord Auckland.

sentiment of fraternity and reciprocal kindness which should accompany such a connexion. These favours seem to be prompted certainly by a liberal, but at the same time, by a wise policy; they are the gifts of an elder to a younger brother; not the wages paid by a superior to a dependant. They ought to excite gratitude, and to improve as well as to secure affection between us; but they need not either exalt the pride of one, or humble that of the other; and, to say the truth, I cannot help feeling that the pride of Ireland may be very well reconciled to an obligation, for which she has the consciousness of returning in the reciprocal blessings of imperial connexion, an ample and corresponding equivalent. I erase, therefore, such topics as these, from my argument of Irish subordination. They appear to me not more inconclusive to that point, than somewhat removed, perhaps, from that liberality which ought to characterize such discussions, whether between individuals or nations; and if these obligations of Ireland to Great Britain are ever enlarged upon, I confess I should see it with more pleasure in Ireland, than in this country.

Those real indications of subordination, on which I mean however to rely, appear to me such as ought not to mortify Ireland; because they are derived from the very nature and constitution of human affairs, and especially from one cause, which must afford, I conceive, rather gratification than disgust to national feeling, I mean the imperial connexion which makes Ireland a member of the noblest empire of the globe. For what, after all, is this imperial connexion in the necessity of which we are all agreed? If it be any thing more than a name, and if it afford any substantial advantage, does it not consist in securing a conformity, or rather a perfect uniformity and unity, in the counsels of the two countries on affairs of imperial concern? Such are, in some respects the regulation of commerce; the transactions and intercourse with foreign states; the declaration of war; the conduct and direction of war; the negociation and conditions of peace. These are the principal, if not all the points of imperial or common concern; and in these it is admitted, and it is manifest that, for common safety and advantage, the two countries must be governed by one mind, and directed by one will, to the same end. Now

let

let me afk in what manner is uniformity to be enfured on points fo much fubject to doubt in themfelves, fubmitted to a judgment, I mean that of the human mind, the variety and uncertainty of which is proverbial, and efpecially where fome degree of temporary and occafional oppofition, both of feeling and intereft, may be looked for in particular feafons and circumftances—I need not go about to prove by any tedious argument, what is always conceded on this point, nor need I fcruple to affert what the beft Irifh patriots, and warmeft partizans of Irifh independence have always freely acknowledged, that unity of counfels can be brought about and preferved, only by leaving the lead to one of thefe nations in thofe points on which it is neceffary that they fhould agree. Every fenfible and enlightened Irifh ftatefman, has, I think, admitted that in imperial concerns, Ireland muft, and ought to follow in the wake of Great Britain. Here then is one authentic and fignal badge of real fubordination. But how is this neceffary acquiefcence of Ireland to be enfured? For it ftands as yet on difcretion and prudence, not on pofitive provifion. May not an interval of paffion, or the fpleen of fome contentious moment, or the influence of fome

popular

popular leader, perfuade Ireland, in an evil hour, to affert her right of feparate and independent deliberation in the common concerns, and to vindicate that right, by fetting up an opinion of her own, different from that adopted in England? Againſt this misfortune, which would otherwife be pretty fure of happening, the conſtitution of our connexion with Ireland has provided fome fecurities. In the firſt place we have the fame King. The King of Great Britain is, in virtue of that crown, King alfo of Ireland. Ireland is content to follow the fortunes of England in that great point; and this I ſtate as another circumſtance of dependence. But there are other ſtill more fenfible tokens of practical fubordination—The whole executive government of Ireland is adminiſtered by a viceroy, appointed indeed by the Sovereign of Ireland, but not with the advice of an Iriſh cabinet. He is appointed, in effect, by a Britiſh Miniſter, he is fubject to inſtructions from a Britiſh Secretary of State, and refponfible for every part of his adminiſtration municipal as well as imperial, not to the Iriſh Parliament, not to the Iriſh Laws, but to the Britiſh Parliament and its high tribunals. Even this is not all; for all this may be thought infepa-

rable

table from the nature and frame of our connexion. There remains a point which was not so much the unavoidable consequence of the imperial constitution, but was thought subject to such a moral and political necessity, as to have been deliberately assented to and retained by the most enlightened and ardent patriots of Ireland, even in the jealous review of her constitution, which took place at that period of enthusiasm and triumph which is become the grand æra of Irish freedom and pride, I mean the year 1782. The circumstance I now allude to is this. The legislative functions of the sovereign of Ireland can be performed only under the Great Seal, not of Ireland, but of Great Britain. Notwithstanding the extreme and jealous tenderness of the Irish nation, on all that could remotely, or even in the refinements of political subtlety, affect the independence of their Parliament; although that Parliament is the shrine on which the nation itself is, it seems, now to be laid a victim; that Irish Parliament was left, and remains at this hour, dependent for the validity of every one of its legislative acts, first on the Chancellor of England, and through his responsibility, on that very Parliament of England,

England, an equal participation in the authority of which is thought so degrading to Ireland. God forbid that Ireland should change her mind on these points of voluntary subordination, or that her pride should supersede her wisdom, and a false dignity take the place of her substantial interests at least in these particulars. For such are the few slender threads which yet hold together these ponderous bodies, and whenever they are broken we part for good. There is yet one other circumstance which not only indicates inferiority, but is so wholly irreconcileable with every notion of equality, and appears to me such a singularity in the condition of any country claiming the character of independent sovereignty, that I must add it to the list before I quit this topic. Ireland must take her part in all the wars of Great Britain. She must bear her share of their burthens, and incur all their hazards. She may lose a province, or may become herself a province of the enemy. Yet Ireland cannot, by the utmost success of the war, acquire an acre of new territory to the Irish dominion. Every acquisition made by the forces of the Empire, however great her share may have been in the danger or exertion, accrues to the Crown of Great Britain. If an island were taken by regiments raised in Ireland, and composed wholly of Irishmen, and by ships manned altogether by Irish seamen, that island is a British conquest and not an Irish one. Ireland claims no sovereignty in any one of the foreign possessions or provinces of the British Empire. She pretends to no dominion in India, in Ceylon, at the Cape of Good Hope, at Martinique, Trinidad, or Minorca. The Irish Parliament has never asserted or conceived the right of legislating for any of the conquests of the King of England, that is to say, of the King of Ireland. They are all subject *ipso facto*, to the Legislature of Great Britain. Ireland has planted no Irish colonies, but has furnished planters to all those of Great Britain. In a word, this whole class of sovereign rights and capacities, however inherent in the very nature of sovereignty, is wholly wanting in that of Ireland. If we were asked to define, or at least to describe an independent sovereignty, should we err much by saying, it is a state which can make war and peace, which can acquire dominion by conquest, and which can plant colonies, and establish foreign settlements? And if we would describe a subordinate

nate and dependent country, could we do it better than by saying, it is a country which must contribute her quota to all the wars of a neighbouring kingdom, must incur all the risks of those wars and partake in all their disasters; while all that is acquired by their success falls, like the lion's share, to that country with which it claims to be co-ordinate and co-equal. I will insist no further on this ungracious topic. What I have said, was necessary for my argument, and if I have demonstrated the real subordination of Ireland, it was certainly not for the disingenuous pleasure of gratifying the vanity of one nation, at the expence of another, but only to observe that subordination must be the constant companion of an imperial connexion with a more powerful and more considerable state, and that pride can fly only to one of two remedies; I mean, total and absolute separation, or a perfect, incorporating and equalizing Union.

This argument is often conducted as if the question lay between distinct existence and total extinction. This is a false view of the alternative. If Ireland foregoes her separate individuality, it is not to perish; but still preserv-

ing

ing in full life and vigour, her own exiſtence, ſhe becomes identified with a larger whole; and ſo far from the pretended annihilation with which our adverſaries would alarm her, ſhe appears to me to acquire new extenſion. I would aſk, in what manner is an inhabitant of any province or county of Ireland degraded, when he is enabled to ſay that he is an Iriſhman, and that he is beſides a citizen of the united empire of Great Britain and Ireland; and when inſtead of admiſſion, as it were, by courteſy, to an indirect and circuitous advantage from the greatneſs of another country, to which he himſelf claims to be in ſome ſort a ſtranger, he can aſſert as clear a title and as poſitive ownerſhip and property in the glory and proſperity of the empire to which he will belong, as any native of Great Britain can do at this moment? I cannot better deſcribe the condition of Ireland after the Union, or better illuſtrate the improvement of its independence and dignity, than by ſaying, that her ſituation will from that moment be preciſely the ſame in all points with that of Great Britain herſelf. Unleſs we ſuppoſe, therefore, Ireland in her preſent ſituation, more independent and leſs ſubordinate than Great Britain, we cannot ima-

gine

gine that her independence will be diminished by the Union. And if it be true, as we have shewn, that she is at present, dependent, and subordinate to Great Britain in many respects, it is clear, that a Union which shall have the effect of placing the two countries on a footing of perfect equality, must improve the independence and dignity of the inferior, that is to say, of Ireland. Is Ireland then annihilated by these means? No; Ireland is still Ireland, while a new scope is given to the pride, and a larger field opened to the patriotism of every Irishman. Let me ask, in fine, where we shall discover in the present condition of Ireland, that superior degree of independent dignity, which should outweigh the real and solid benefits of Union; or where we can perceive in the change which that Union will operate on the political situation of Ireland, the degradation and indignity which should forbid her even to deliberate, and raise an insuperable barrier, both to her aggrandizement and happiness?

I do conceive, indeed, how the situation of some individuals may be such as to afford a greater share of personal consideration or advantage

vantage in Ireland, while confined within its prefent limits, than they might obtain on the greater theatre of the united kingdoms. Even here, indeed, the computation may be fallacious; but however that queftion may ftand with regard to individuals, I am fure that the inhabitants of Ireland will gratify a found love of national dignity, while they procure to their country unfpeakable advantages of every other fort, by their acceffion to the noble empire of which the Union would make them citizens.

I muft therefore conclude, that although I muft refpect the feelings of thofe who, following this inftinct of national pride, which I have allowed to be in fome fort natural, have been blinded to the true merits of this queftion, either as it regards the interefts or the dignity of their country; and, although I cannot refufe a confiderable degree of indulgence, even to the intemperance and violence excited by any form of patriotifm, and even by its errors; yet I muft perfift in faying, that thofe will ever appear to me to have evinced a more genuine, a more profound and folicitous affection for their country, who have not refufed to deliberate

liberate on such mighty interests, but have resisted a first and false impulse, and chosen for their guide rather the slower and less captivating torch of reason, than the more lively flashes of passion and prejudice. Nor can I refrain from adding, that if there be indeed any individuals, or descriptions of men, who not misled themselves, but far above the influence of those delusions which they have practised upon the multitude, have seen nothing in this great question but personal or local interests, and have sought to mask a narrow preference of individual and partial advantage, under this pretence of national pride and feeling; if such men, I say, with these motives at the bottom of their hearts, and with the profanation of a great public virtue on their lips, have frustrated the wise and paternal counsel given by our common Sovereign for the permanent and perpetual benefit, and not less for the present and immediate preservation of the empire in all its parts, and especially of their own particular country; I own I cannot part with this subject, without declaring loudly, that I envy, neither the pillows and consciences of those men, nor the place they are likely to fill in the history of their country.

There is yet one objection on which I am disposed to trespass on your Lordship's indulgence, rather from the importance which has been given to it by those who oppose the Union, than from any weight I think it entitled to myself. The point I now allude to, is a supposed disability in the respective Parliaments of Great Britain and Ireland to sanction such a measure.

This is another objection on which the merits of the main question are waved, and in which those who have been defeated on that ground, or who are conscious that they must be so, would still take refuge. It resembles a plea to the jurisdiction; and, although I am far from assenting to a very absurd doctrine which I have heard falsely ascribed to our law, that he who pleads to the jurisdiction shall abide by that plea; and when it has been over-ruled shall not plead over, but be concluded on the facts and merits of his cause; yet I think myself entitled to claim thus much from those who resort to this objection. That, although after it has been over-ruled, and the jurisdiction of Parliament has been established, they shall be at liberty to recur back to the

question

question of expediency; yet, while we are discussing the question of competence, and for the purpose of that argument, the merits shall be granted. The objection cannot otherwise be placed on its own proper and peculiar ground. For, if the competence of Parliament were disputed merely on the ground of inexpediency in the particular act, it must be felt in a moment that the question of competence with regard to the Union, would stand exactly on the same footing as if it related to any other legislative measure, however clearly within the acknowledged powers and daily practice of Parliament. In order to obtain, therefore, a distinct and substantive judgment on the question of competence, it must be kept pure; and uncomplicated with any other consideration; which can only be done by trying it in a case of admitted expediency. I think myself entitled, then, for the purpose of this argument, to assume, that the proposed Union would be beneficial to both countries, and I am at liberty to state its advantages, or its necessity as high as I please. In a word, my adversary in this argument must assent to the measure as expedient and necessary, denying, only, the authority of Parliament to execute it.

Now, if a measure be expedient, I am to ask, in the first place, why may it not be executed by Parliament? and, in the next place, if Parliament is not competent, where shall we find a more adequate authority? I have, for me, the general rule and law of the Constitution, which establishes the universal authority of the Legislature, and defines it by no limits or qualification that I am acquainted with. Whatever the whole nation could do, if there were no Parliament, is within the regular and fundamental powers of Parliament. This is admitted to be the general rule; and here I might plant my foot, at least until the exception were specified, and the principle of that exception established. The universality of Parliamentary power has been characterized by the strong and emphatic title of Omnipotence. And, in the theory of our Constitution, strong and emphatic as this phrase is, it need not, I think, be deemed, merely a bold figure, as it has been called by some writers on our Government, but as literally and correctly descriptive of parliamentary supremacy, and of the unlimited sovereignty of the British Legislature.

I am

I am aware of the reply generally made to this affertion of unlimited power. I may be told, that powers unlimited in theory, are yet finite and controuled in practice, and that, in its exercife, the moft unbounded authority is ftill circumfcribed, at leaft within the moral boundaries of right and wrong. I affent to this reftriction, and even affert it; but what does my adverfary gain by this conceffion? Parliament ought not to do what is wrong, and is to be fuppofed incapable of doing it. In this fenfe, the power of Parliament, is no more limited than the Divine Omnipotence itfelf, which is incapable of evil. I fay alfo of Parliament, that it is incapable of evil; and I fay it in this fenfe, that what Parliament does is not to be accounted evil, but is to be taken and acquiefced in as right—Why? will it be faid. Is not Parliament compofed of men, and therefore fallible? Yes—but who muft judge the fallibility of Parliament, and to whom muft its queftionable acts be fubmitted—if it be not to other men, yet more fallible than themfelves? For I wifh to know where men are to be found, or in what forms or combinations they are to be affembled, to whom

fuch

such a superlative authority could with safety be confided.

The more we turn this argument, and the more carefully it is viewed on all its sides and bearings, the more we shall be satisfied, that the only security we possess for every thing valuable in the British Government; that all that conduces to order and happiness; that the whole efficacy of our Constitution towards its great and beneficial purposes, resides in this single principle, of the unlimited, unqualified, supremacy of Parliament. There is no appeal, acknowledged in the Constitution, from that authority, because no appellate tribunal can be imagined, habile to such a jurisdiction; none from which the wisdom of those many ages, which have brought our Constitution to maturity and excellence, has not already constituted an appeal, final and conclusive in all cases whatever, to that very Parliament, from which you would, again, appeal back to them. Observe the vicious circle into which this appeal from the Parliament to the People must lead us. The people at large cannot conveniently, nor safely for themselves, make law, or

administer

administer Government. The Constitution of Parliament has therefore been framed, as affording the most commodious and perfect organ of Law and Government, and the best and most secure depositary of the sovereign authority. But their acts must, it seems, be questioned, and their authority superseded by that very people at large, whose inability and unaptness have given occasion to the institution of Parliament. The speedy resolution of the argument into this contradiction and absurdity, is, therefore, manifest.

It is easy to foresee that this claim of unlimited power may be opposed by the counter-claim of a right to resist an abuse and perversion of authority, however legal. This question of resistance, that is to say, concerning the right of the subject to oppose by force, the act or orders of the legal sovereign, by which your Lordships know, I should not mean, in this country merely the throne, but that I speak of that body in which the full sovereignty of any nation resides, according to the established Constitution of its Government, and which, with reference to this kingdom, would be the Parliament; the point, I say, thus explained,

of

of refiftance, at the difcretion of the fubject, to the legal fovereign, is of no trivial concern, and ought not to be rafhly or irreverently approached. The queftion is of high import, and delicate complexion. It appears to me, to be one of thofe myfteries, the acknowledgment of which is much connected with its recluse fanctity, and its being withdrawn from daily and vulgar contemplation, to be referved only for the great occafions which are worthy to draw it forth, and, "*like a robe pontifical,* " *—ne'er to be seen, but wondered at.*" I believe it is impoffible that any thing better fhould be faid on this fubject, than what I find quoted by an eloquent patriot of my own country, Mr. Fletcher, of Saltown, from the mouth of Mr. William Colvin, whom he ftiles one of the wifeft men Scotland ever had, and who, fpeaking of defenfive arms, that is to fay, the right of the fubject to carry arms, for the purpofe of refifting oppreffion from the Sovereign, was ufed to exprefs himfelf in thefe remarkable words : " That it were to be wifhed " all Princes thought them lawful, and the " People unlawful. No wifh can be more falutary, and no anfwer to this delicate and important queftion can be more perfectly wife as well as difcreet. I confefs, alfo, that on this fingle fubject, I do not like the folution the worfe for being fomewhat oracular.— But if a peremptory opinion be demanded, and we muft needs pronounce, I think myfelf entitled to anfwer generally in the language of the conftitution. No limit has been appointed to the authority of the fovereign; nor any exception fpecified to the obedience of the fubject. The conftitution has not forefeen any cafe of refiftance, and has made no provifion for it. Such a cafe is not, and cannot be, in the contemplation of any conftitution whatever. A pre-eftablifhed, that is to fay, a conftitutional right of refiftance to the conftitutional fovereign is a folecifm; a mere contradiction in terms. It can exift in no conftitution that either is, or ever was, becaufe it is inconfiftent with the very notion of conftitution, or government. We muft anfwer, then, that refiftance is illegal, and is contrary to the law, in every form of government of which law is the foundation. If an extreme cafe be put to me, I may well refufe to anfwer it, until the cafe arife in practice. Stated theoretically, it is always a fnare. When it happens practically the cafe will anfwer for itfelf; and

if

if refiftance would not follow on the fpur of any provocation that can be ftated, without the previous fanction of fome declared, and anticipated authorization in the conftitution to legalize it, it is a cafe which we may pronounce, by that very criterion, unfit to produce or juftify refiftance. Every cafe of refiftance muft ftand as it were upon its own individual refponfibility, and muft be fuch as to provide for itfelf, without the aid of any antecedent principle to lean upon. Such cafes, whatever may be faid of them by hiftory, whatever may be felt of them by the generous fympathies of mankind, muft look for no fupport from law, with which they cannot coexift ; they are all without the pale of law and all illegal ; they are all extra-conftitutional ; all in direct contradiction with the particular conftitution, as well as with the general principle of government ; they are mere folitary, infulated, fubftantive facts, equally incapable of deriving from, or generating any binding analogy of general and permanent authority. Thefe queftions are not new in this country. We have paffed through a century of fuch controverfies, and have, fince that period, enjoyed a century more of happinefs, the fruit of

the

the wife and profound, as well as spirited judgment of our anceftors on thefe debates; a judgment, as your Lordfhips know, equally removed, on one hand, from a mean and pufillanimous acquiefcence under oppreffion, and on the other from thofe fhallow but ruinous abftractions which fo much pains are taken to bring once more into fafhion. We do not come, therefore, in England, fo raw into thefe difcuffions, as to be mifled by the juvenile refinements of political metaphyfics, or by the early puerilities of thofe who may have read their Locke without reading hiftory, or who in reading their Locke have forgot their hiftory, into errors, which we know to be as fatal to the practical bleffings of liberty, as to the ftrength and ftability of government. We know that an eftablifhed fyftem and theory of refiftance is but another word for anarchy; and that, whatever be the excellence of any conftitution in other refpects, however wifely and fkilfully conftructed it may be, even for ftability, in its other provifions, let there be added this one principle of a permanent and fubfifting right to refift, even in the moft limited cafe, fince the exiftence of that cafe muft, by the very nature of the thing, be fubmitted to the difcretion of every individual in the ftate, that conftitution will bear in its bofom the feed of its own diffolution, and a principle of difperfion and demolition, utterly irreconcileable with the tranquillity or peace of the people, and deftructive of all tenacity and duration in the government.

But it will be faid, this is not a queftion of refiftance, and we are enquiring only whether this meafure does not exceed the limits of that authority with which the conftitution has invefted Parliament.

I am then, to afk, fince the power of Parliament is general and undefined, in what refpect is this particular act diftinguifhable from others which are admitted to be within its competence, in fuch a manner as to become an exception to the general rule of the conftitution. And here I am under the difficulty of thofe who are to combat without an adverfary, or to combat an adverfary whom they cannot fee. I am to fearch for my opponent, or muft begin by creating the enemy whom I am afterwards to engage. For as yet I have certainly heard nothing precife on this fubject. I muft,

I muſt, therefore, look amongſt the diſtinctive qualities of this meaſure, for ſome circumſtance on which to found the exception. The firſt circumſtance I obſerve in the Union of two countries, is an extenſion of territory, compared with the former bounds and ſurface of each, ſince each is reſpectively augmented by the acceſſion of the other. But this effect of Union cannot be a ground of diſqualification to Parliament, ſince the conſtitution commits the ſame power to a narrower authority. I mean the prerogative of the Crown alone. If a conqueſt be made without any contrary ſtipulation, the conquered country becomes ſubject, *ipſo facto*, to the Legiſlation of Parliament. The King may alſo obtain by treaty the annexation of any new territory to his Crown, by which means it will fall, of courſe, under the Government of the Britiſh Parliament. In both theſe ways the dominion of Great Britain can be enlarged, to any extent, by the ſole prerogative of the Crown—and much more by the King in Parliament. We muſt look, then, for ſome other circumſtance in this caſe to exclude the general authority of Parliament.

Beſides

Besides extending the bounds of the kingdom, at present subject to the sovereignty of Parliament, a Legislative Union extends and enlarges Parliament itself, accommodating the size of the Legislature to the accession of territory. It amounts then to an alteration in the frame and condition of Parliament; and we are to enquire whether Parliament is, on that account, disqualified from performing it.

It may be worth while to remark, in the first place, that this formal change is however consonant with the general spirit and genius of the Constitution. Is it not fair, while we are discussing the conditions under which two countries are to be united, to consider what would have been the case if they had been one from the beginning? Would not Ireland, in that case, have had representatives in the Legislature? It would not be difficult to shew from history, that while Ireland was considered as exclusively under the Government of the English Parliament, that is to say, before the institution of the Irish Parliament, that country sent members to the Parliament of England. The same principle has generally, though

I do

I do not fay without exception, operated in fimilar cafes, I mean in cafes of the acceffion of contiguous territories. Of this, Wales, the Counties Palatine, and Scotland, are familiar examples. The minor inftances of Calais, and Berwick on Tweed, may have been lefs attended to, but they illuftrate alfo this general propenfity of our Conftitution. While Calais was fubject to the Crown of England, that town enjoyed and exercifed, by charter from Harry the Eighth, the privilege of fending two burgeffes to Parliament. And as foon as Berwick on Tweed, which being a frontier town, frequently changed mafters according to the various fortune of war, was at length fettled under the dominion of England, by the union of both Crowns, and the final extinction of war, at the acceffion of James the Firft, that town received alfo the franchife of returning members to Parliament. The Conftitution, in a word, leans that way: and it may, perhaps, reafonably be thought a greater violence to that Conftitution, and a more fundamental and effential change, to add extenfive territories to the country already governed by Parliament, without giving to thofe territories a participation in the Conftitution, and a fhare in

the

the reprefentation, than to accompany 'fuch an acceffion of territory with a legiflative as well as an incorporating union. Yet, no man difputes the power of the Crown, according to the prerogative which I have lately ftated, to operate the former and the greater change even without the aid of Parliament. It is not, then, fair to argue, *a fortiori*, and *a multo fortiori*, that the larger authority of the whole Legiflature, fhall be more competent, or much more competent, to the fmaller change, that is to fay, to extend the bounds of the empire in a manner congenial and in unifon with the Conftitution, as it would do in the meafure propofed, than the narrower power of the prerogative can be to the greater change, that is to fay, to an acceffion of territory and an union with other countries, on a principle abhorrent from the genius of our Government. Yet the competence of thefe latter acts, whether to the Crown or to the Parliament, has never been difputed; and refts, indeed, too firmly on the repeated and ordinary exercife of their powers to admit of queftion.

But let us return to this objection, and admit, that a Legiflative Union with Ireland,
muft

must operate a change on the condition, or even on the Constitution of Parliament; and let that change be as considerable as the objector would chocfe to state it. Does it follow that such a change on Parliament cannot be made by Parliament, as it may be said in physics, that a body cannot act upon itself? Such an alteration appears to me, neither more nor less than a law, and as such, to fall within the natural province of the law-giver, who, in this country, is the Parliament. How will it be shewn that these laws, affecting the Constitution of Parliament, are alone incompetent to Parliament? Our own experience has taught us the contrary. I dare say there are very few of your Lordships who have not assisted in the passing of laws precisely of this description, and, however warmly such measures may have been resisted or debated on other grounds, I will venture to say, there is not one of us who has ever heard or known this objection, of the insufficiency of Parliament, opposed to them. The various laws for limiting the duration of parliaments, for regulating elections, for altering the qualification of electors, or elected, for disfranchising offending boroughs, and communicating their franchises to strangers, that

is

is to say, for example, to the freeholders of a neighbouring hundred; all these, and many more, falling precisely within the principle of this objection, have been passed, by no higher authority than that of Parliament. What are all those proposals for what is called sometimes moderate, sometimes radical reform, but laws for the alteration, for the total subversion of the Constitution of Parliament? To me they have appeared little short of revolution, incipient revolution. Yet, I have never heard one of those, who with similar views of these projects, have been better qualified, than myself, by talents and weight in this country, to oppose them, object the incompetence of Parliament to entertain and to adopt these changes in its own Constitution, if they should appear expedient.

An alteration of the established religion, which has always been the work of Parliament, is another change, and a most fundamental one in its Constitution; since the whole parliamentary franchise, whether elective or representative, is transferred from one class and description of the people to another. The

whole

whole is taken from all those who possessed it, and vested in those who did not.

The laws so frequently made by Parliament for altering and regulating the succession to the Crown, bears a strong analogy to the case which is now objected to, amounting, indeed, to a total change in one whole branch or member of the Parliament.

This objection, then, cannot be maintained *simpliciter*, on the incompetence of Parliament to make an alteration on its own constitution, or condition; and we must come, in fine, to the single point which my imagination can suggest, as a possible ground of distinction, namely, the great and superlative importance and magnitude of this transaction. We have seen that all other cases of a similar nature, *ejusdem generis*, are within the acknowledged powers of Parliament, and the daily exercise of those powers. But this is a measure, we must say, of such transcendent importance, as to exceed the ordinary capacities entrusted by the Constitution to Parliament, and to which the inherent sovereignty of the people itself is alone commensurate.

I can conceive no other rational shape into which this argument can be cast; but is it rational in substance also; or is it not the most palpable and the grossest violation of reason, the widest departure from every sound principle in the theory either of this constitution, or of government in general? It would be strange indeed if this point of superior importance should serve my adversary, since it is the very ground on which I rest most firmly my claim of exclusive cognizance to the Parliament.

On what principle is the trust of legislation committed to Parliament at all? Because no people on earth, not even the smallest population in the smallest territory, could ever exercise a democratic legislation in its entire and theoretical purity. If we look back to that most antient and simple of all constitutions, I mean the patriarchal, or the government of families, which has been regarded as the first, and original model and archetype of all succeeding governments, we shall find that even these have rejected a mode of administration which it was, at least, easier to execute, within the walls of a single tent, or the bounds of a wandering camp, and amongst a few individuals,

viduals, than in any other more populous state. Authority was still deposited with selection in fewer hands than the whole even of these narrow communities. The heads of families; the chiefs of tribes; the elders; in a word, some select body or other, administered these small commonwealths. It would lead to unprofitable length if I were to pursue this reasoning with minuteness, as it would be easy to do, up to the conclusion, to which we all assent; namely, that the people of England cannot make law for themselves in any democratic form of constitution; that they are not provided or acquainted with any institution which should enable them to perform this feat of self-legislation, even if they were desirous of attempting it. They have no comitia; no assemblies of the people in Hyde Park, or St. George's Fields, to the decrees of which the millions of absent Englishmen, owe, or choose to acknowledge any obedience. And there being a physical impossibility to collect their voices individually, even if that physical and practical impossibility, if I may say so without the imputation of incorrectness, were not the weakest objection to such a mode of legislation, there is an established organ of the general will,

will, qualified by its frame and conſtitution, to apply the collective wiſdom of the nation to its collective intereſts, and to adminiſter the ſovereign power of the ſtate on this ſecure and ſolid foundation. The ſovereignty of Parliament, thus explained, is in the end no more; it is neither more nor leſs, but identically and preciſely the ſame with the ſovereignty of the people itſelf, appearing in the only viſible, tangible or perceptible form in which it can be recognized in this country.

It is, then, firſt, on the vices and inabilities of all other modes by which the voice of the people can be expreſſed, or even its opinions formed agreeable to their general and collective intereſts; and ſecondly, on the peculiar and approved excellence of the Conſtitution which we enjoy, that the authority and ſovereignty of Parliament has been eſtabliſhed.

Let us endeavour, for a moment, to imagine ſome better mode of collecting, in a popular way, the ſenſe of the nation, on any great point of policy or law, or, if you pleaſe, on this ſpecific meaſure. Shall it be by meetings convoked by anonymous hand-bills, in the fields

adjoining

adjoining to this metropolis, and directed by orators on carts, tubs, or other moveable roſtra? Every one knows that an Union with Ireland, for the diſcuſſion of which ſuch aſſemblies were to be called, would not be the firſt order of the day. The moſt preſſing ſympathies and fellow feelings of ſuch a legiſlature would be for the ſuffering felons, traitors, or mutineers, in Newgate and Cold-bath-fields. Their firſt and ſecond meaſures, in favour of the liberty and property of the ſubject, would be to deliver the gaols, and emancipate the bank; and they would ſoon ſimplify this intricate and complex Conſtitution, by uniting the legiſlative, the judicial, and the executive powers; as they would abridge the tedious delays of all thoſe functions, by carrying, with their own hands, into inſtant effect, their own laws and judgments. I remember to have ſeen a Parliament deliberate in St. George's-fields in the forenoon; and I do not forget, that on the ſame evening I ſaw London and Weſtminſter in flames. Shall the appeal from Parliament lie to county-meetings, called by the ſheriffs, on the requiſition of a few dozens of ſignatures; and ſhall the people of England be bound in this great intereſt, by a collation of

the

the various and discordant resolutions, passed by a respectable shew of hands, at the different Georges and Angels of the kingdom? Shall the magistrates at quarter-sessions, shall grand juries at assizes; or, in fine, shall the church-wardens and overseers of the poor at parish vestries, supersede Parliament, on account of their superior wisdom and knowledge; and, above all, because they have received a more authentic and direct delegation from the people at large? Or shall we prefer, rather, those convivial parliaments which hold their sittings occasionally at the different taverns of this city? whose resolutions, moved in the form of toasts, are agreed to in bumpers; and whose laws, proposed in stanzas, to the tune of a ballad, are passed in full chorus. Is not this jovial system of legislation, a mere inversion of the good old Constitution, which, if it permits the electors to be drunk, requires the Parliament to be sober? But must we, then, to speak seriously, depose the Parliament chosen by the people, in favour of these self-elected, self-balloted parliaments, attended by every small minorities of that Parliament which was chosen by the people, after they have withdrawn their attendance from that Parliament

to

to which the people sent them? In fine, what is to be the form of this Arch-Parliament, which is to qualify it better than the British Parliament, as it now stands, for legislating, just in proportion as the subject is of higher import and dignity, and of greater compass and difficulty, than those ordinary acts of legislation to which those high authorities are utterly inadequate and incompetent?

Is it not, then, manifest, that a legislature in which the sovereignty of the State is vested, because every other political body, known in this country, is deficient in the requisites for common and ordinary legislation, and because it is itself the most perfect model of human polity, in all matters of legislation, must be yet better entitled to preference and to exclusive and sovereign jurisdiction, in cases of great and signal importance, than in any other? It seems to me, therefore, the strangest perversion of reason, and the most palpable contradiction and absurdity, to place the incompetence of Parliament on that ground on which its sole and exclusive competence most firmly and securely rests; I mean the superior importance of this law.

Having

Having spoken to the principle, let us see how the question stands on authority.

I shall not encumber my argument with the authorities which are familiar in every mouth, to prove a position, not disputed in any quarter, namely, the general supremacy of Parliament; and I shall respect your Lordships' leisure sufficiently to omit the book authorities on this general but fundamental truth, although the passages I might refer to, assert distinctly, as your Lordships know, amongst other examples of the universal faculties of Parliament, its competence to this specifick measure of a legislative Union with other countries.

There are two sorts of authority: First, the opinions of learned and eminent men. Next, precedent.

To begin with the first, and to speak of the *responsa prudentum*.

To the learning of the corporations of Dublin, and of the freeholders of the county of Louth, and some other counties; to the authority

thority of some members of the Irish bar, I shall oppose the Chancellor of Ireland, and the Chiefs of the four Supreme Courts of Law in that country. I shall oppose the clear and unequivocal sense of the House of Lords of Ireland, evinced not only by its vote, but by the withdrawing that part of the amendment, proposed originally by Lord Powerscourt, which involved that question. I shall oppose the opinion of the majority of the House of Commons of Ireland, for I think myself entitled to claim the dissent of that House to this proposition on a fair and candid view of its proceedings. The House once agreed, by a majority, however slender, to entertain the measure; and afterwards rejected it by a majority as slender; for the difference between one and five hardly deserves notice. If to this equality of opinion on the principal measure be added the consideration that the opposers of the Union did not even tender this proposition to the House; did not venture to load their question, with that denial of the competence of Parliament, of which it had been found necessary actually to relieve the same question in the House of Lords, we shall hardly doubt of their consciousness, that in a balance trimmed so nicely, this weighty point would have turned the scale against them. But as time adds sanction and reverence to authority, let me close this enquiry by opposing to all the rash and intemperate opinions, or rather declarations of opinion, which the temerity of party spirit, or a false and misguided enthusiasm, have dictated in Ireland at this day, the single authority of Lord Somers; himself, I think, a host, on such a question. If any man in England, or in Ireland, as has been often said of that great man, think himself a better Lawyer or a better Whig than Lord Somers, he is welcome to enter the lists; while I shall rest contented with this single name, supported as it might be by a cloud of learned, able, and upright statesmen, lawyers, and friends of liberty from that period to the present hour.

Let us now look at precedent. It is not to be expected that there should be many. Such transactions must be rare. It is enough for my argument, to say, that the only examples our history furnishes, of Legislative Unions, since the institution of Parliaments, are precedents in point on the question I am now debating; namely the competence of Parliament to enact

enact them. WALES and SCOTLAND have both been united to England by incorporating, Legiflative Unions. In both cafes the Parliament alone fanctioned the meafure. The union with Scotland is, perhaps, yet more clofely in point with the prefent propofal. Since a feparate Parliament exifted in both countries, and the refpective Parliaments were the parties in the treaty. That treaty was negotiated under the authority of the two Parliaments; they fanctioned the conclufion; and they executed finally and irreverfibly, that happy fyftem, under which we now live fecure, at the diftance of almoft a century.

Although our hiftory cannot furnifh many precedents of this precife meafure, I mean, of incorporating Unions, there are, however, many examples of other proceedings, bearing a ftrong anology to the prefent, and equal, if not fuperior, in importance. I mean thofe acts of the Legiflature which have altered the fucceffion to the Crown. I need not cite the inftances of fuch changes. They are frequent in the Hiftory of England, and they all prove the fupreme authority of Parliament, even in thefe higheft acts of fovereignty. By whatever

ever means fuch changes have been brought about; whatever has been the efficient caufe, or inftrument of fuch revolutions, they have all derived their fanction and validity from Parliament, the feal of which has always been reforted to by the new Sovereign, as the only effectual fecurity for his title, whether he ftood on a claim effentially good, or on fuccefsful ufurpation. And the anxiety with which the many repetitions of parliamentary recognition have been fought after, by thofe who were interefted in a new or queftionable title, is remarkable on this argument.

But without dwelling on more antient examples, it is furely fufficient to recall that of the Revolution, which placed King William on the Throne, and the fubfequent limitation of the Crown to the Houfe of Hanover. Will it be faid, that the declaration of King James's abdication, and the vacancy of the Throne, was a point of lefs note or value, or of a lower rank in the fcale of fovereign functions, than tha Union with Scotland, or Wales, or than the meafure now in contemplation? Will it be faid, that the whole tranfaction of the Revolution was of a lower or meaner clafs and order,

order, in legiflation, than any Union, or any other national event that is either known or can be imagined. I do not fear that it will.— By what authority, then, was that great change in one branch of the Legiflature, and in the condition of the nation, operated? To what authority was the Prince of Orange advifed to refort, for the fanction of his enterprize and the fecurity of his Crown? Obferve the difference between the circumftances in which he ftood, and thofe in which the prefent proceeding is tendered to Parliament. By the flight and abdication of the King, and the confequent vacancy of the Throne, an actual and practical diffolution of the Government feemed to have taken place, if it can ever do fo, in any poffible or imaginable cafe. It was in fuch a predicament, if it could happen in any, that the fuppofed dormant title of the people to adminifter the fovereignty in their own perfons, fo far at leaft as regarded the reintegration of the deficient and truncated Government, muft have been awakened and called into action. That moment was, indeed, different from the prefent, in which we have every branch of the Legiflature complete, and the whole frame of our Government not only

perfect

perfect and apt to all its purposes, but in the actual and daily exercise of its functions; and in which we are ourselves debating this very question concerning parliamentary powers, within the walls of a subsisting Parliament, and in the ordinary discharge of our parliamentary duty. Yet, under the circumstances which I have described, what did the Prince of Orange resolve, under the direction of his whig advisers? Did he apply to the people at large in any new and anomalous form? Was it to county meetings, or assemblies in the fields, or, in a word, to any unknown and unusual organ of the public mind, that he applied to sanction his title? Far from it. Even the first Convention, under the authority of which he afterwards summoned the Convention Parliament, was composed, in the first place, of the House of Lords; and next, of those who had been members of Parliament in the reign of Charles the Second. It will not be said, that these persons had any specific delegation from the people, either for this special act, or for any other end; either express, by positive commission, or implied, by their recent election. A whole reign had elapsed since they came from the people. Their delegation and functions

had

had been exhausted and had expired long since. Yet, so much preferable did this approximation to the regular constitutional authority, when an entire conformity with it was impossible; so much preferable did even this shadow, this surviving flavour of the parliamentary character, which still hung about these relics of a deceased Parliament, appear, when compared with any new and strange invention for conjuring up the latent sovereignty of the people, and substituting some phantom and chimera to represent that sovereignty in the room of its only true and acknowledged form, I mean that of Parliament, that the Prince of Orange did not think the validity of a Convention Parliament, to be summoned by his new authority, would stand on a sure foundation, until its convocation should receive the sanction, if not of a subsisting Parliament, at least of a body as nearly and closely resembling one as the circumstances admitted. The Convention Parliament was convoked—and that Parliament enacted the Revolution—which, however, was hardly yet deemed perfect, until it was consummated by the ratification of subsequent and yet more regular Parliaments.

The

The subsequent limitation of the Crown, after the death of the Duke of Gloucester, was also the work of Parliament; and I believe so far from deeming that authority incompetent, or wishing to rely on any other higher or more transcendent power, none of those whig statesmen and lawyers who presided in every step of the revolution, and who had the protestant succession at heart, would have thought that great object secure, if the limitation to the Princess Sophia had stood on a decree of the people, conveyed by any other organ than precisely that which they employed, I mean the Parliament. If these great men, then, were content to rest the revolution itself, that vast and prime concern, embracing every other possible interest of Englishmen, on the single and perfect efficacy of an Act of Parliament, we are not to wonder if the same men thought the respective Parliaments of England and Scotland, the competent, and the only competent instruments to accomplish the Union between the two countries.

What overweening preference is it of our own times, or our own persons, that should make us thus fastidious in casting by, or of inferior

ferior and more imperfect growth, the constitutional whiggism and wholesome liberty of the reigns of King William and Queen Ann, to intoxicate ourselves and our country with that double refined, that sublimated and adulterated modern drug which is now poisoning the world. I own, for my part, that I like to see, on the liberty of my country, and your Lordships know the revered authority by which I am supported in that sentiment, that I like to see on my own and my country's liberty the seal of the old whigs, and am apt enough to think that counterfeit, which does not bear this mark. I am above all disposed to fly as from certain ruin, the spurious philosophy, the sophisticated, and fatal abstractions, which so far from lighting us to the temple of liberty, are but decoys to plunge the world into the toils of wretchedness and slavery. I confess, then, that I recoil with disgust and not without alarm, from every pretence for disavowing or superseding our established government, however qualified in time, occasion or limited purpose. I cannot think those men profitable servants of their country, nor do I think their country disposed to regard them as friends, who would weaken in the breasts of

English-

Englishmen the native and rooted love of our boasted government and laws; and divert the settled allegiance of the happiest people upon earth, from the established sovereignty of Parliament, in which, however, is inseparably bound up the whole of the security, prosperity and freedom, present and to come, of the British nation. And I must hold every proposal to abdicate or surrender the sovereign power of Parliament, but for an hour, into the hands of any strangers to the constitution, that is to say, into any other hands whatever, as a mere fraud upon the people; as a gross violation of its most precious privilege; as a flagrant invasion of the dearest birth-right of Englishmen, which consists according to me in the right to be governed by their Parliaments, and by no other human means.

There are a variety of topics, as your Lordships well know, to which I have not even alluded, and on some of which I should certainly be disposed to say a few words; but, in truth, I have already abused your indulgence, not only much too long, but, I am conscious, also, much too tediously; and I therefore refrain—very grateful for having been permitted

to

to state such reasons as have satisfied my mind, on the whole matter, that this measure is expedient in itself, and that Parliament is competent to execute it. I have expressed a strong opinion, that the Union of these two nations, already united by nature in their interests, must, in the order of human events, necessarily come to pass; and I shall conclude by a sincere and fervent prayer, dictated by the purest and the most ardent desire for the happiness of both kingdoms, that the blessings sure to flow from a consummation so devoutly to be wished, may not be long delayed.

FINIS.

www.ingramcontent.com/pod-product-compliance
Lightning Source LLC
Chambersburg PA
CBHW030336170426
43202CB00010B/1143